The Southern Cook

The Southern Cook

The Very Best of Southern Cooking

First published by Parragon Inc. in 2013
LOVE FOOD is an imprint of Parragon Books Ltd

Parragon Inc.
440 Park Avenue South, 13th Floor
New York, NY 10016
www.parragon.com/lovefood

ISBN: 978-1-4723-1117-7

Printed in China

Project Managed by Kerry Starr
Written by Margaret Agnew
Photography by Sian Irvine
Home Economy by Korrie Bennett
Cover designed by Talking Design

Notes for the Reader
This book uses standard kitchen measuring spoons and cups. All spoon and cup measurements are level unless otherwise indicated. Unless otherwise stated, milk is assumed to be whole, eggs are large, individual vegetables are medium, and pepper is freshly ground black pepper. Unless otherwise stated, all root vegetables should be washed in plain water and peeled prior to using.

For best results, use a food thermometer when cooking meat and poultry. Check the latest USDA government guidelines for current advice.

Garnishes, decorations, and serving suggestions are all optional and not necessarily included in the recipe ingredients or method.

The times given are only an approximate guide. Preparation times differ according to the techniques used by different people and the cooking times may also vary from those given. Optional ingredients, variations, or serving suggestions have not been included in the time calculations.

Recipes using raw or very lightly cooked eggs should be avoided by infants, the elderly, pregnant women, convalescents, and anyone with a weakened immune system. Pregnant and breast-feeding women are advised to avoid eating peanuts and peanut products. People with nut allergies should be aware that some of the prepared ingredients used in the recipes in this book may contain nuts. Always check the packaging before use.

Vegetarians should be aware that some of the prepared ingredients used in the recipes in this book may contain animal products. Always check the package before use.

Picture acknowledgments
The publisher would like to thank the following for permission to reproduce copyright material:
Clive Streeter: pages 17; 22; 49; 52; 87; 116; 144; 149; 156; 166; 167
Rob Streeter: pages 14; 40; 68; 100; 112; 117; 148; 157; 185; 193
Charlie Richards: pages 29; 76; 78; 90; 94; 98; 136; 153; 182
All other incidental images courtesy of iStock Images

Contents

Introduction

Pull up a chair to a Southern dining table, and count yourself lucky. For a good meal shared with a true Southern family is an experience not to be missed. Not only will you be treated to a feast guaranteed to delight your taste buds, but you will also enjoy a generous helping of hospitality and be welcomed into the family fold like a long-lost cousin. Soft drawling voices set against the tinkling of ice in glasses of tea will provide the backdrop for good conversations…"That sure was a hard rain we had today." "Are ya'll going to the game (football, of course) this weekend?" or, "My tomato plants are already three feet high!" You might be referred to as "Sugar" or "Darling," and will probably not escape without a fond "bless your heart." It's all part of the Southern dining experience.

Being Southern has always had more to do with a state of mind and being, and less with what state you were born in or where you actually lived. But some people like to draw boundaries. For those, the South, sometimes referred to as "Dixie," is generally defined as the area from the Atlantic Seaboard and the Gulf Coast of the Southeastern United States, to the Appalachian Mountains and south of the Mason-Dixon Line (a demarcation drawn below the states of Pennsylvania, Maryland, Delaware, and West Virginia). Looking westward, the area is marked by the Ozark Mountains and the states of Texas and Oklahoma.

The food of the Southern states is traditionally comprised of pork, beef, fish, chicken, and turkey, an abundance of fruits and vegetables, lots of sauces and gravies, fragrant herbs and spices, breads made from both corn and flour, flavorful whiskies, and an endless array of desserts—cookies, cakes, pies, puddings, ice creams, and various fruity concoctions. Grits, cornbread, and whiskey are by-products of Indian maize. Pork and puddings were brought by Spanish and English explorers. Peas and greens and sweet potatoes came from Africa. Rice, spices, and most fruits came to the South via the Orient. Rich gumbos, jambalayas, and étouffées came from Louisiana's French Cajuns and Creoles.

In days gone by, Southern diners enjoyed a full menu of traditional favorites every day, sometimes twice a day at both lunch and dinner or supper as it was often called. But over time,

Being Southern has always had more to do with a state of mind and being, and less with what state you were born in or where you actually lived.

most Southern families have adjusted menus and taken a healthier approach. However, even today, when holidays or special occasions roll around, nothing is held back. There will typically be at least one main entrée, multiple fresh vegetables, cornbread or biscuits still warm from the oven, and definitely a buffet laden with desserts.

It used to be that every Southern community had its well-known cooks—this kind of news quickly spread by word-of-mouth, and sometimes the best cooks even won blue ribbons at local county fairs. These homegrown talented cooks earned a reputation for baking the best cake or frying the best chicken or canning the perfect jam or jelly. In the New South, our communities now have well-known professional chefs, even James Beard winners, most of whom have earned their fame by creating dishes that feature fresh produce and local ingredients.

Southern food has given pleasure in good times and bad.

Early Southern family life revolved around food and the growing seasons. Whether they gathered to grind grain, to marry, to bury the dead, to barter, to play games, or to pray, food was always at the center of life. As a result, food began to symbolize Southern culture and traditional Southern hospitality.

Even today, food remains the language that ties Southern communities together. Whenever there is a festival, fair, or a political or religious event, folks often collect around an open-pit fire to take turns flipping quarters of chicken, pork shoulders, or ribs. On bake sale tables you might find bags of boiled peanuts, tall frosted coconut cakes, moist peanut butter cookies, and sweet potato pies.

The Southern tradition of sharing large quantities of good food and drink with friends and strangers has proved to be enduring. Whether the family was rich or poor, the ultimate gathering spot in the Southern home was the dining room, for this is where guests were greeted with the finest their hosts could offer.

On the great plantations, the food presented on the mansion

dining table was far more elaborate than in the houses of most ordinary Southerners. Meals for African slaves might have been prepared in the central kitchen, but more probably, their meals were cooked in their cabins in a pot in their fireplace. And the slaves had a great influence on Southern food. From them came dishes using okra, black-eyed peas, collard greens, yams, and benne seeds. They originated the recipe for beaten biscuits and a long list of impressive desserts.

The aftermath of the War between the States and the Great Depression left the South poor. Food was scarce and times were hard. With almost no money for food, Southern families had to be resourceful. They taught each other what they knew about cooking. They learned how to make rich gravy from fat and flour, how to turn stale bread into pudding, and how to stretch a minimum of vegetables into a soup or stew. They planted, harvested, cooked, baked, canned, and preserved what they could.

No doubt about it, Southern food has given pleasure in good times and bad. The food has survived African slavery, Indian exile, war, and severe economic poverty. Now, it is even withstanding the popularity of modern restaurants and fast food. Almost the opposite of fast food, Southern food is prepared slowly, from scratch with fresh ingredients, and carefully seasoned with just the right spices and flavorings. It can be rich, but it can also be mouthwatering and nutritious. That is why some adaptations and subtle changes have been made in recent years to old recipes, in order to accommodate beneficial diet and health needs.

In addition, as family life has become busier and work and other pursuits outside the home and farm have increased and become more demanding, clever Southern cooks have sometimes streamlined favorite family dishes passed down to them from their grandmothers and mothers, occasionally substituting canned or frozen ingredients in order to make them quicker and easier to prepare. To be sure, old-fashioned Southern cooking no longer dominates the daily diet of the Southern people like it used to. But make no mistake, the love of the people for genuine, traditional Southern cookery remains. Great Southern food is too wonderful to ever forget.

Recipes

Spring

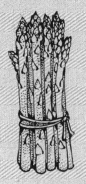

WHOLE CARAMELIZED ONIONS

Southerners are fond of onions and use them in salads, meat dishes, soups, casseroles, and breads. Here is a time-honored way to bake onions so that they cook up tender and sweet.

YIELD: 4–6 SERVINGS

INGREDIENTS

1½ pounds medium-size onions, peeled
¼ cup unsalted butter or margarine
½ cup firmly packed brown sugar
¼ cup light corn syrup
½ teaspoon salt

1 Arrange onions on a steaming rack, and place over boiling water; cover and steam for 20 minutes, or until tender. Drain onions and place in a lightly greased 8-inch-square baking dish.

2 Melt butter in a saucepan over low heat. Stir in sugar, syrup, and salt, and bring to a boil over medium heat. Reduce heat, and simmer for 5 minutes. Pour glaze over onions; cover and bake at 350° for 25–30 minutes.

FRIED DILL PICKLES

Fried pickles rose to popularity in Arkansas and Mississippi and are now enjoyed throughout the South. They are eaten as an appetizer and are frequently served with a creamy ranch-type sauce for dipping.

**YIELD: ABOUT
2½ DOZEN**

INGREDIENTS

1 quart dill pickles,
thinly sliced
1⅔ cups all-purpose flour
2 teaspoons red pepper
2 teaspoons black pepper
1 teaspoon salt
1 cup beer
vegetable oil

1 Place pickles in a zip-top plastic bag; add 1 cup flour, and shake until all slices are coated. Combine remaining ⅔ cup flour, red pepper, black pepper, and salt in a mixing bowl; add beer, mixing well. Dip dredged pickles into beer batter.

2 Deep fry pickles in hot oil (375°) until pickles float to surface and are golden brown. Drain on paper towels; serve immediately.

CHEESE WAFERS

Southern social gatherings and teas just aren't complete without a silver tray of cheese straws or cheese wafers. The addition of red pepper gives these little rounds a nice warm bite.

YIELD: 4–5 DOZEN

INGREDIENTS

2 cups (8-ounces) shredded sharp cheddar cheese, softened

½ cup unsalted butter, softened

1¾ cups all-purpose flour

¾ teaspoon cayenne pepper

⅛ teaspoon salt

pecan halves

1 Combine cheese, butter, flour, cayenne, and salt; mix until blended. Shape dough into two long rolls; wrap in wax paper and refrigerate at least 3 hours.

2 Remove rolls from refrigerator, unwrap, and cut into ¼-inch slices; place on ungreased baking sheets. Mash a pecan half in center of each wafer. Bake at 350° for 12–15 minutes, or until lightly browned. Cool on wire wracks.

MINTED SUGAR SNAPS

Sugar snap peas can be steamed, stir-fried, or served in salads. If not ultra fresh and tender, they may need to be "stringed" by removing the thin membrane running along the top of the pod from base to tip.

YIELD: 4 SERVINGS

INGREDIENTS

½ pound fresh sugar snap
pea pods

2 tablespoons unsalted
butter or margarine

1 large red bell pepper, cut
into ¼-inch strips

3 tablespoons chopped
green onions

1 tablespoon chopped
fresh mint

¼ teaspoon salt

1 Wash sugar snaps; trim ends and remove strings, if desired. Set aside.

2 Melt butter in a large skillet. Add sugar snaps and remaining ingredients; stir gently. Cover and cook over medium-high heat for 6–8 minutes, or until pods are crisp-tender. Serve immediately.

MARINATED ASPARAGUS SPEARS

Asparagus requires patience to grow; after planting, it takes two or three years before the plant begins to produce. The good part is that the stalks cook very quickly—in just a matter of minutes.

YIELD: 4 SERVINGS

INGREDIENTS

1 pound fresh, thin asparagus spears

Marinade
¼ cup cider vinegar
¼ cup vegetable oil
½ teaspoon salt
¼ teaspoon white pepper
¼ teaspoon garlic powder
2 tablespoons diced pimiento
1 tablespoon minced fresh parsley

1 Snap off tough ends of asparagus. Cook asparagus, covered, in boiling water for 4–6 minutes or until crisp-tender. Drain well and arrange spears in a shallow dish.

2 Combine marinade ingredients, stirring well. Pour marinade over asparagus; cover and refrigerate overnight. Serve with a slotted spoon.

NEW POTATOES IN CREAM SAUCE

During lean times, Southern cooks always served potatoes, since they were easily grown in home gardens. Their families found them delicious mashed with butter or served whole and tossed in a rich cream sauce.

YIELD: 4 SERVINGS

INGREDIENTS

12 small new potatoes

3 tablespoons unsalted butter or margarine

3 tablespoons all-purpose flour

½ teaspoon salt

¼ teaspoon white pepper

1 cup milk

½ cup half-and-half

1 tablespoon chopped fresh chives

1 Wash potatoes; pare a 1-inch strip around center of each potato. Place potatoes in a large saucepan; cover with water and bring to a boil over medium heat. Cover, reduce heat, and simmer for 15–20 minutes, or until potatoes are tender; drain well.

2 Melt butter in a heavy saucepan over low heat; add flour, salt, and pepper, stirring until smooth. Cook for 1 minute, stirring constantly. Gradually stir in milk and half-and-half; cook over medium heat, stirring constantly, until thickened and bubbly. Pour over potatoes; sprinkle with chives.

SPRING SPINACH SALAD

Fresh, tender spinach makes a lovely salad. Here the leaves are combined with spring strawberries and dressed with a vinaigrette.

YIELD: 4–6 SERVINGS

INGREDIENTS

1 pound fresh tender spinach
leaves
1 pint fresh strawberries,
washed, hulled, and halved

**Sesame Strawberry
Vinaigrette**
½ cup sugar
2 tablespoons sesame seeds,
toasted
1½ teaspoons grated onion
¼ teaspoon Worcestershire
sauce
¼ teaspoon paprika
½ cup vegetable oil
¼ cup cider vinegar or
strawberry vinegar

1 Remove stems from spinach leaves and wash leaves thoroughly. Pat leaves dry and tear into bite-size pieces. Combine spinach and strawberries in a large bowl, tossing gently.

2 Combine vinaigrette ingredients in container of an electric blender; cover and process at low speed for 30 seconds. Drizzle Sesame Strawberry Vinaigrette over salad; toss gently.

ENGLISH PEA SALAD

English peas are often served hot with butter and black pepper for Sunday dinner. But the tiny peas can also be stirred into a creamy, chilled salad for a ladies luncheon or covered dish dinner.

YIELD: 6–8 SERVINGS

INGREDIENTS

2 (17-ounce) cans English peas, drained, or
3 (10-ounce) packages frozen tiny green peas, thawed
2 cups finely chopped celery
1 (8-ounce) can sliced water chestnuts, drained
1 (4-ounce) jar diced pimiento, drained
½ cup chopped green onions
½ cup sour cream
½ cup mayonnaise
¼ teaspoon salt
¼ teaspoon white pepper

1 Combine peas, celery, water chestnuts, pimiento, and green onions in a large bowl. Combine sour cream and mayonnaise, stirring well. Add sour-cream mixture, salt, and pepper to vegetables; toss gently to coat. Cover and chill thoroughly.

CHICKEN SALAD IN MINIATURE TOAST CUPS

Good Southern hostesses master the art of making chicken salad. Here the salad is served in dainty toast cups, but it can also be spread on slices of soft bread and turned into a sandwich.

YIELD: 70 FILLED TOAST CUPS

INGREDIENTS

1 loaf thinly sliced white or whole wheat bread
unsalted butter or margarine, softened
1 cup finely chopped cooked chicken
½ cup finely minced celery
¼ cup finely chopped pecans, toasted
1 teaspoon honey mustard
1 teaspoon lemon juice
mayonnaise
salt and black pepper to taste

1 Roll bread slices flat with a rolling pin. Lightly butter one side of each slice of bread. Cut each slice into four 2-inch rounds, removing crusts, using a small cookie or biscuit cutter. Press rounds into miniature muffin pans, buttered side up. Bake at 325° for 10–15 minutes, or until lightly browned. Remove from pans and cool completely.

2 Combine chicken, celery, pecans, honey mustard, and lemon juice, stirring gently. Add enough mayonnaise to moisten chicken mixture. Season with salt and pepper. Fill toast cups before serving.

CUCUMBER TEA SANDWICHES

These tiny sandwiches are the ultimate finger food and are served at all kinds of events, from tea parties for dolls to grown-up wedding showers and elaborate receptions.

YIELD: 40 APPETIZER SANDWICHES

INGREDIENTS

½ small onion, coarsely chopped

2 (8-ounce) packages cream cheese, softened

½ teaspoon salt

¼ teaspoon ground white pepper

1 teaspoon minced fresh dillweed or ¼ teaspoon dried dillweed

80 slices thin white or whole wheat bread

1 large cucumber, peeled and thinly sliced

2 (3-ounce) packages cream cheese, softened

2–3 teaspoons milk

tiny sprigs of fresh dillweed (optional)

1 Place onion in container of food processor fitted with a metal blade and process until finely minced. Cut 2 (8-ounce) packages cream cheese into 1-inch pieces. Add to processor and process until smooth. Add salt, pepper, and 1 teaspoon dillweed; process until blended.

2 Cut bread slices into rounds, removing crusts, using a 2½-inch biscuit cutter. Spread about 1 tablespoon of cream cheese mixture on 40 of the bread rounds. Arrange cucumber slices over cream cheese mixture. Top with remaining bread rounds.

3 Combine 2 (3-ounce) packages cream cheese and milk in a small bowl; mix until smooth. Spoon cream cheese mixture into a decorating bag fitted with a rosette tip; pipe a rosette of cream cheese on top of each sandwich. Garnish each sandwich with a sprig of dillweed, if desired.

GLAZED VIRGINIA COUNTRY HAM

Virginia reigns as the most famous producer of country hams. Genuine country hams can be purchased cooked or uncooked; they are salt-cured, slowly smoked, and sold in burlap bags.

YIELD: 25–35 SERVINGS

INGREDIENTS

1 (12–14-pound) uncooked country ham

1 quart apple cider

2 cups apple juice

2 cups orange juice

whole cloves

2 cups firmly packed brown sugar

2 tablespoons water

1 Place ham in a very large container; cover with water and soak 24 hours to remove excess salt. Pour off water. Scrub ham in warm water with a stiff brush and rinse well.

2 Drain ham; place in a large roasting pan. Pour apple cider, apple juice, and orange juice over ham; add enough water to cover. Insert a meat thermometer into ham making sure it does not touch fat or bone. Bring juice mixture to a boil; cover, reduce heat, and simmer gently 3–4 hours or until thermometer registers 142°. Drain ham and let cool thoroughly. Discard pan juices.

3 Trim skin from ham. Score fat in a diamond design and stud with cloves. Return ham, fat side up, to roasting pan. Pat 1½ cups brown sugar over ham. Combine remaining ½ cup brown sugar and 2 tablespoons water in a small saucepan; cook over medium heat, stirring until sugar dissolves. Brush ham with sugar glaze. Place in oven and broil 5 inches from heat for 5 minutes or until sugar caramelizes.

HONEY-GLAZED HAM

This ham is so moist and delicious that each slice practically melts in your mouth. The sweet outer coating teams nicely with the saltiness of the ham.

YIELD: 12–14 SERVINGS

INGREDIENTS

1 (6–8-pound) smoked, fully cooked bone-in ham half

⅔ cup firmly packed brown sugar

⅓ cup sugar

1½ teaspoons ground nutmeg

1 teaspoon ground cloves

½ teaspoon ground cinnamon

½ cup honey

1 Remove hard outer skin from ham, leaving a thin layer of fat; place ham, fat side up, on a rack in a shallow roasting pan. With a sharp knife, score fat in a diamond design; insert meat thermometer into ham, making sure it does not touch fat or bone. Bake at 325° for 1 hour and 15 minutes. Remove ham; leave oven on.

2 Combine brown sugar, sugar, nutmeg, cloves, and cinnamon, stirring well. Brush ham generously with honey. Pat brown-sugar mixture over honey, coating ham thoroughly. Return ham to oven, and bake at 325° for 30–40 minutes, or until meat thermometer registers 140°.

BEST BARBECUED RIBS

Good barbecued ribs are revered in the South. All barbecue experts have tips to share, but two of the best are to cook ribs over a slow fire and to add the sauce during the last 30 minutes of cooking.

YIELD: 3–4 SERVINGS

INGREDIENTS

4 pounds pork back ribs or spare ribs
1 tablespoon paprika
1 teaspoon salt
1 teaspoon black pepper
1 teaspoon garlic powder
1 teaspoon cayenne pepper
¼ cup catsup
¼ cup red wine vinegar
¼ cup tomato sauce
2 tablespoons honey mustard
1 tablespoon Worcestershire sauce
1 tablespoon unsalted butter or margarine
1 teaspoon hot sauce
1 teaspoon lemon juice
1 teaspoon brown sugar
½ teaspoon salt
¼ teaspoon garlic powder
⅛ teaspoon chili powder
⅛ teaspoon cayenne pepper
⅛ teaspoon black pepper
½ cup red wine vinegar
½ cup water
1 tablespoon brown sugar

1 Place ribs in a large, shallow roasting pan. Combine paprika, 1 teaspoon salt, 1 teaspoon pepper, 1 teaspoon garlic powder, and 1 teaspoon cayenne pepper in a small bowl; stir well. Rub spice mixture over ribs. Cover pan with aluminum foil and refrigerate ribs for 4 hours or overnight.

2 In a small saucepan, combine catsup, ¼ cup red wine vinegar, tomato sauce, honey mustard, Worcestershire sauce, butter, hot sauce, lemon juice, brown sugar, ½ teaspoon salt, ¼ teaspoon garlic powder, chili powder, ⅛ teaspoon cayenne pepper, and ⅛ teaspoon pepper; bring to a boil. Reduce heat, and cook, stirring often, 15–20 minutes. Set sauce mixture aside.

3 Bake ribs, covered, in oven at 300° for 1 hour. Drain ribs.

4 Heat a charcoal or gas grill. Combine ½ cup red wine vinegar, water, and brown sugar, stirring well. Grill ribs, covered with grill lid, over medium coals (300°–350°) for 10–15 minutes, basting with vinegar mixture and turning ribs frequently.

5 Brush ribs with barbecue sauce mixture; continue to grill ribs, uncovered, for 10–15 minutes or to desired degree of doneness, turning ribs occasionally and brushing heavily with sauce mixture.

PAN-GLAZED RAINBOW TROUT

The creeks, streams, and rivers of the Appalachian Mountains provide fly fishermen with solitude and a bounty of fish. The best part of a fisherman's day is when he savors his catch.

YIELD: 2 SERVINGS

INGREDIENTS

2 whole, cleaned rainbow trout (about 1½ pounds)
¼ cup all-purpose flour
½ teaspoon salt
½ teaspoon black pepper
⅛ teaspoon paprika
⅛ teaspoon garlic powder
4 tablespoons unsalted butter, melted
¼ cup slivered almonds
1 teaspoon brown sugar

1 Rinse fish under cold water; pat dry.

2 Combine flour, salt, pepper, paprika, and garlic powder in a large bowl. Dredge fish in flour mixture; shake off excess. Fry fish in 2 tablespoons melted butter in a large cast-iron skillet for 5 minutes on each side, or until golden. Transfer to a serving dish.

3 Add remaining 2 tablespoons butter to skillet. Add almonds and brown sugar; cook, stirring constantly, until almonds are golden. Spoon almonds and butter-sugar glaze over fish. Serve immediately.

BLACK BEANS & RICE

Southerners love simmered beans and peas—red beans and rice in Louisiana, Hoppin´ John in South Carolina, and black beans and rice in Florida. Start with dried beans, or when in a hurry, use canned beans.

YIELD: 8–10 SERVINGS

INGREDIENTS

1 pound dried black beans

1 large green pepper, chopped

1 large onion, chopped

4 cloves garlic, minced

2 to 3 tablespoons olive oil

¼ cup dry white wine

2 tablespoons vinegar

1 teaspoon salt

½ teaspoon black pepper

hot cooked yellow rice

chopped green onions

1 Sort and wash beans; place in a large Dutch oven. Cover with water 2 inches above beans; let soak overnight.

2 Sauté green pepper, onion, and garlic in olive oil until tender; stir mixture into beans. Add wine, vinegar, salt, and pepper, stirring well. Cover and bring to a boil; reduce heat, and simmer 1½–2 hours or until desired degree of doneness, adding more water, if necessary. Serve over hot cooked yellow rice; top with chopped green onions.

SHRIMP & GRITS CASSEROLE

Your opinion of simple grits will soar when you sample this wonderful casserole. It can be served for a real casual family dinner, but it is also elegant enough for a fine dinner party.

YIELD: 8 SERVINGS

INGREDIENTS

2 tablespoons butter or margarine
6 green onions, chopped
1 green bell pepper, chopped
1 clove garlic, minced
4 cups chicken broth
1 cup quick-cooking grits
2 cups shredded cheddar cheese
1 (10-ounce) can mild tomatoes and green chiles, drained
1 pound small or medium shrimp, cooked and drained
¼ teaspoon salt
¼ teaspoon black pepper
¼ cup fine, dry bread crumbs

1 Melt butter; sauté onions, green pepper, and garlic until tender.

2 Bring chicken broth to a boil. Gradually add grits, stirring with a wire whisk until smooth; cook for 5 minutes or until thickened.

3 Add cheese, tomatoes, onion and green pepper mixture, salt, pepper, and shrimp, stirring until combined. Spoon into a lightly greased 13- x 9- x 2-inch baking dish. Sprinkle with bread crumbs. Bake at 350° for 30–35 minutes or until bubbly and lightly browned.

MARINATED BEEF TENDERLOIN

When Southern cooks need an impressive main course, they often turn to beef tenderloin. This lean cut of meat looks nice served over a bed of rice or surrounded with cooked fresh vegetables.

YIELD: 8–10 SERVINGS

INGREDIENTS

1¼ cups port wine
½ cup vegetable oil
¼ cup lemon juice
¼ cup Worcestershire sauce
¼ cup water
2 teaspoons black pepper
1 teaspoon dried thyme leaves
1 teaspoon hot sauce
4 cloves garlic, crushed
1 bay leaf
1 (5–6-pound) beef tenderloin, trimmed

cooked fresh vegetables

1 Combine wine and next 9 ingredients in a large shallow dish or zip-top freezer bag; add meat. Cover tightly, and refrigerate at least 8 hours, turning meat occasionally.

2 Remove beef from marinade, reserving marinade. Heat marinade in a small saucepan until it comes to a full boil; discard bay leaf. Set marinade aside.

3 Place tenderloin in a roasting pan. Bake at 425° for 40–45 minutes, or until a meat thermometer registers 140° (rare), basting occasionally with marinade. Remove meat to serving platter; serve on a bed of fresh vegetables with marinade.

ARKANSAS ROASTED CHICKEN

Some delicious poultry dishes are shared at the Annual Poultry Festival held each year in Rogers, Arkansas, but it's hard to improve upon the flavor of simple roasted chicken, a favorite throughout the South.

YIELD: 4 SERVINGS

INGREDIENTS

1 (5-pound) whole roasting chicken

salt

⅓ cup unsalted butter or margarine, softened

1½ teaspoons chopped fresh marjoram or ½ teaspoon dried marjoram

¼ teaspoon hot sauce

Tips

Fresh chicken should be kept covered in a refrigerator for no more than three days— longer storage increases bacteria count. Wash thoroughly before cooking. Use a separate cutting board for preparing raw chicken, and wash hands and utensils carefully.

1 Remove giblets and neck from chicken; reserve for other uses. Rinse chicken with cold water and pat dry. Lift wing tips up and over back so they are tucked under chicken. Sprinkle chicken cavities with salt. Tie ends of legs together with string; set aside.

2 Combine butter, marjoram, and hot sauce; spread over chicken. Sprinkle lightly with additional salt. Place chicken, breast side up, in a shallow roasting pan. Bake at 375° for 2 hours, or until a meat thermometer inserted into thigh registers 180°, or until drumsticks are easy to move up and down, basting often with pan drippings. Remove to a serving platter.

PASTA-RICE CASSEROLE

Rice has a rich Southern history and has been grown in South Carolina, Arkansas, Louisiana, and east Texas. This casserole adds nice texture to menus and teams well with green beans and fried chicken for Sunday lunch.

YIELD: 6 SERVINGS

INGREDIENTS

⅓ cup unsalted butter or margarine
3 ounces spaghetti, broken into small pieces
1 cup regular long-grain rice, uncooked
1 teaspoon chicken-flavored bouillon granules
2 cups water
1 cup chicken broth
⅓ cup chopped green onions
1 (8-ounce) can sliced water chestnuts, drained

1 Melt butter in a large skillet. Add spaghetti; sauté over high heat until golden, stirring constantly. Remove from heat.

2 In a large bowl, combine sautéed spaghetti and remaining ingredients. Pour into a lightly greased 8-inch-square baking dish. Bake at 350°, uncovered, for 40–50 minutes. Stir gently before serving.

SORGHUM TEA COOKIES

Sorghum grows in stalks that yields juice when pressed. The juice is boiled down to make sorghum syrup, which can be used as a substitute for molasses or sugar or as a topping for hot biscuits or pancakes.

YIELD: 8–9 DOZEN

INGREDIENTS

1 cup unsalted butter, softened

¾ cup sugar, plus extra for sprinkling

3 eggs

1 cup sorghum syrup

2 tablespoons buttermilk

6–7 cups all-purpose flour

1 teaspoon baking soda

2 teaspoons ground cinnamon

1 Cream butter on low speed of an electric mixer; gradually add sugar, beating on medium speed until light and fluffy. Add eggs, one at a time, beating well after each addition. Add sorghum syrup and buttermilk. Mix well.

2 Combine flour, soda, and cinnamon. Stir dry ingredients into creamed mixture. Cover dough and refrigerate for 8 hours or overnight.

3 Roll dough out to ¼-inch thickness on a lightly floured board; cut with a 1½-inch cookie cutter. Place cookies on a lightly greased baking sheet. Sprinkle lightly with sugar. Bake at 375° for 8–10 minutes, or until golden brown; cool on wire racks.

DAINTY COFFEE WAFERS

These delicate cookies are a modern invention, made with a cookie press, and are perfect for serving at teas or parties. You will be rewarded with smiles of delight.

YIELD: ABOUT 5 DOZEN

INGREDIENTS

¼ cup plus 2 tablespoons unsalted butter or margarine, softened

½ cup sugar

2 tablespoons milk

2 tablespoons instant coffee granules

1 egg

½ teaspoon vanilla extract

2¼ cups all-purpose flour

1 teaspoon ground cinnamon

1 Cream butter on low speed of an electric mixer; gradually add sugar, beating at medium speed until light and fluffy. Combine milk and coffee granules, stirring well. Add coffee mixture, egg, and vanilla to creamed mixture, beating well.

2 Combine flour and cinnamon; add to creamed mixture, mixing well.

3 Press dough from a cookie press onto ungreased baking sheets, making 2-inch ribbon-like strips. Bake at 400° for 6 minutes or until edges are lightly browned. Remove from baking sheets and let cool completely on wire racks.

JULIETTE GORDON LOW COOKIES

Perhaps this thin, sesame seed cookie was the original Girl Scout cookie, since they are named after Juliette Gordon Low, founder of the Girl Scouts, who was born in Savannah, Georgia.

YIELD: ABOUT 10 DOZEN

INGREDIENTS

¾ cup butter or margarine, softened
1½ cups firmly packed brown sugar
2 eggs
1¼ cups all-purpose flour
¼ teaspoon baking powder
½ cup sesame seeds, toasted
1 teaspoon vanilla extract

1 Cream butter on low speed of an electric mixer; gradually add sugar, beating well. Add eggs, one at a time, beating well after each addition.

2 Combine flour and baking powder in a small bowl; add to creamed mixture, beating well. Stir in sesame seeds and vanilla.

3 Drop dough by teaspoons 2 inches apart onto parchment paper-lined cookie sheets. Bake at 325° for 12–15 minutes. Cool completely on cookie sheets. Remove from parchment paper, and store in an airtight container.

MODERN BEATEN BISCUITS

True beaten biscuits require much time and effort—some old recipes suggested that the dough be beaten vigorously at least 200 times. Thankfully, this version has been adapted to make use of the convenient food processor.

YIELD: ABOUT 2 DOZEN

INGREDIENTS

2 cups all-purpose flour
1 teaspoon sugar
½ teaspoon salt
½ teaspoon baking powder
½ cup solid vegetable shortening, chilled
¼ cup half-and-half
¼ cup ice water

1 Place flour, sugar, salt, and baking powder in a food processor fitted with a metal blade. Cover and process for 1 second to mix. Add chilled shortening; cover and process 5–6 seconds, or until mixture resembles coarse meal.

2 With food processor running, add half-and-half and ice water in a stream through the food chute. Process until dough forms a ball. Continue processing for 2 additional minutes.

3 Turn dough out onto a lightly floured board. Roll dough out to ¼-inch thickness; fold dough over on itself to make 2 layers. Cut dough with a 1¾-inch biscuit cutter; place on an ungreased baking sheet. Prick each biscuit 2 or 3 times with the tines of a fork. Bake at 350° for 30 minutes or until biscuits are lightly browned.

DERBY PECAN TARTS

There are many traditions associated with the Kentucky Derby. One of them is serving these tarts at pre-race parties and celebrations.

YIELD: 2 DOZEN TARTS

INGREDIENTS
1 cup all-purpose flour
¼ teaspoon salt
1 (3-ounce) package cream cheese, softened
½ cup unsalted butter, softened

Pecan Filling
¾ cup firmly packed brown sugar
1 teaspoon unsalted butter, softened
1 egg
¼ teaspoon salt
1 teaspoon vanilla extract
¾ cup chopped pecans

1 Combine flour and salt; add cream cheese and butter, mixing until a soft dough forms. Refrigerate dough for 1 hour.

2 Shape dough into 24 balls; place each in a lightly greased miniature muffin pan, pressing to form a shell. Bake at 350° for 10–15 minutes or until lightly browned. Let cool.

3 Combine remaining ingredients for filling, mixing well. Spoon 1 teaspoon filling mixture into each pastry shell. Bake at 350° for 10–15 minutes or until golden and set.

PRALINE CHEESECAKE

Each bite of this cheesecake brings to mind the flavor of pralines. First the crust is baked, then the filling, and finally the topping, so that it becomes a thrice-baked cheesecake.

YIELD: 8 SERVINGS

INGREDIENTS

1¼ cups graham cracker crumbs

3 tablespoons brown sugar

¼ cup unsalted butter or margarine, melted

3 (8-ounce) packages cream cheese, softened

1 cup firmly packed brown sugar

1 tablespoon all-purpose flour

3 eggs

1 teaspoon vanilla extract

1 teaspoon liquid butter flavoring

1 (16-ounce) container sour cream

¼ cup brown sugar

¼ teaspoon liquid butter flavoring

Chopped toasted pecans

1 Combine graham cracker crumbs, 3 tablespoons brown sugar, and butter; stir until blended. Press crumb mixture evenly over bottom and up sides of a 9-inch springform pan. Bake at 350° for 5 minutes. Let cool.

2 Beat cream cheese on high speed of an electric mixer until light and fluffy; gradually add 1 cup firmly packed brown sugar and flour, mixing well. Add eggs, one at a time, beating well after each addition. Stir in vanilla and 1 teaspoon butter flavoring. Pour mixture into prepared pan. Bake at 375° for 45 minutes, or until set. Remove from oven.

3 Combine sour cream, ¼ cup brown sugar, and ¼ teaspoon butter flavoring; stir well. Spread sour cream mixture evenly over baked cheesecake. Bake at 500° for 5 minutes. Let cool to room temperature on a wire rack. Refrigerate cheesecake for at least 8 hours before serving. Decorate with pecans.

TWO-CRUST SLICE O' LEMON PIE

The Shakers wasted very little, thus they used the entire lemon in this pie. The recipe captures just the right mix of sweet, but tart taste. If you have a mandolin, use that to slice the lemon into paper-thin slices.

YIELD: 6–8 SERVINGS

INGREDIENTS
Double-Crust Pie Pastry (*page 166)
1⅓ cups plus 1 tablespoon sugar
2 tablespoons all-purpose flour
¼ cup unsalted butter, softened
3 eggs
½ cup water
1 medium lemon, peeled and sliced paper-thin
1 egg white

1 Line a 9-inch pie plate with half of pastry and set aside.

2 Combine 1⅓ cups sugar and flour, stirring well. Cream butter on low speed of an electric mixer; gradually add sugar mixture, beating until light and fluffy. Add eggs, one at a time, and ½ cup water, beating well. Stir in lemon slices; spoon into prepared pastry.

3 Roll remaining half of pastry to ⅛-inch thickness and place over filling. Trim edges of pastry; seal and flute edges. Cut slits to allow steam to escape; brush with egg white and sprinkle with remaining 1 tablespoon of sugar. Bake at 400° for 30–35 minutes.

FESTIVAL STRAWBERRY PIE

Strawberries from Florida appear in markets each year by February, and the National Strawberry Festival rolls out the red carpet in Plant City, Florida, in March. This pie is typical of the fine recipes the festival produces.

YIELD: ONE 10–INCH PIE

INGREDIENTS

3 egg whites
1 cup sugar
1 teaspoon vanilla extract
1 cup finely crushed pretzels
1 cup chopped pecans
1 cup whipping cream
2 tablespoons powdered sugar
2 cups strawberries, sliced
whole strawberries

1 Beat egg whites until soft peaks form. Gradually add sugar and vanilla, and beat until stiff peaks form. Fold in crushed pretzels and pecans. Spread mixture in a greased 10-inch pie plate, spreading sides higher. Bake at 350° for 30 minutes or until lightly browned. Cool shell completely.

2 Beat whipping cream until foamy; gradually add powdered sugar, beating until soft peaks form. Fold in sliced strawberries. Spread mixture evenly in shell. Decorate with whole strawberries. Chill pie for at least 4 hours before serving.

LEMON MERINGUE PIE

Lemon meringue pie ranks with pecan pie as one of the oldest and most popular pies in the South. This is the perfect way to make the tart, meringue-topped concoction.

YIELD: 6–8 SERVINGS

INGREDIENTS
Single-Crust Pie Pastry
(*page 152)
1⅓ cups sugar
½ cup cornstarch
1¾ cups water
4 eggs, separated
3 tablespoons unsalted butter
or margarine
1 tablespoon grated lemon
rind
¼ cup lemon juice
½ teaspoon cream of tartar
¼ cup sifted powdered sugar

1 Line a 9-inch pie plate with pastry; trim and flute edges. Bake at 450° for 12–14 minutes or until lightly browned. Let cool.

2 Combine 1⅓ cups sugar and cornstarch in a heavy saucepan. Gradually add 1¾ cups water, stirring until smooth. Cook over medium heat, stirring with a wire whisk until mixture thickens and comes to a boil. Boil for 1 minute, stirring constantly. Remove from heat.

3 Beat egg yolks on high speed of an electric mixer until thick and lemon-colored. Gradually stir about one-fourth of hot sugar mixture into beaten egg yolks; add egg yolks to remaining hot mixture, stirring constantly. Cook over medium heat, stirring for 2–3 minutes. Remove from heat. Add butter, lemon rind, and lemon juice; stir until butter melts; keep warm.

4 Place egg whites and cream of tartar in a large bowl; beat on high speed of an electric mixer until foamy. Gradually add powdered sugar, 1 tablespoon at a time, beating until stiff peaks form and sugar dissolves.

5 Spoon warm lemon filling into baked pastry. Immediately spread meringue over filling, sealing to edges of pastry. Bake at 325° for 25–30 minutes, or until top is browned and set, shielding edges of pastry with aluminum foil if pastry browns too quickly. Let pie cool for several hours before slicing. Store pie in refrigerator.

Tips

Either wash thoroughly or buy unwaxed or organic lemons if you want to use the peel. You can get more juice from a lemon if you warm it for a few seconds in the microwave or in hot water, before squeezing.

EASY JELLY ROLL SWIRL

Jelly rolls have always been a much-loved favorite in the South. Rather than being frosted, the cake is topped with a dusting of powdered sugar.

YIELD: 10 SERVINGS

INGREDIENTS

4 eggs

¾ teaspoon baking powder

½ teaspoon salt

1 cup sugar

1 cup all-purpose flour

1 teaspoon vanilla extract

powdered sugar

1 cup raspberry or strawberry jelly

whipped cream (optional)

1 Grease a 15- x 10- x 1-inch jelly-roll pan and line with wax paper; grease and flour wax paper. Set aside.

2 Combine eggs, baking powder, and salt; beat on high speed of an electric mixer until foamy. Gradually add 1 cup sugar, beating until thick and lemon-colored. Fold in flour and vanilla extract. Spread batter evenly in prepared pan. Bake at 400° for 10–12 minutes, or until top of cake springs back when touched.

3 Sift powdered sugar in a 15- x 10-inch rectangle on a dish towel. When cake is done, immediately loosen from sides of pan and turn out onto sugar. Peel off wax paper. Roll cake and towel up together. Cool cake rolled in towel, seam side down, for about 15 minutes.

4 Unroll cake; remove towel. Spread cake with jelly and reroll. Place on serving plate, seam side down. Cool completely. Serve with whipped cream, if desired.

BANANA PUDDING

Banana pudding is widely enjoyed in the South. It has tempting layers of bananas, vanilla wafers, yellow pudding, and golden meringue.

YIELD: 6 SERVINGS

INGREDIENTS

½ cup sugar
3 tablespoons brown sugar
3 tablespoons cornstarch
¼ cup water
2 eggs, separated
1½ cups milk
1 teaspoon vanilla extract
20–25 vanilla wafers
2 medium bananas, sliced
⅛ teaspoon cream of tartar
2 tablespoons powdered sugar

1 Combine sugar, brown sugar, and cornstarch in a heavy saucepan, stirring well. Add ¼ cup water; mix well.

2 Beat egg yolks; add milk and mix well. Gradually stir milk mixture into sugar mixture. Cook over medium heat, stirring constantly, until mixture comes to a boil. Boil for 1 minute, stirring constantly, until thickened. Remove from heat and stir in vanilla. Set aside to cool slightly.

3 Arrange half of vanilla wafers in bottom of a 1½-quart baking dish; spread with half of pudding. Top with banana slices. Arrange remaining vanilla wafers around the outside edge of dish. Top with remaining pudding mixture.

4 Combine egg whites and cream of tartar. Beat on high speed of an electric mixer until foamy. Gradually add powdered sugar, beating until stiff peaks form. Spread meringue over pudding, sealing to edge of dish. Bake at 325° for 20 minutes, or until golden brown.

PINEAPPLE UPSIDE-DOWN CAKE

There are many variations of this cake, which is baked in a cast-iron skillet, including apple and cherry, but pineapple is the most traditional. After baking, the warm cake is inverted onto a plate so that the glazed fruit becomes the top.

YIELD: 6 SERVINGS

INGREDIENTS

½ cup unsalted butter or margarine

1 cup firmly packed brown sugar

1 (20-ounce) can pineapple slices, undrained

7 maraschino cherries

12 pecan halves

3 egg yolks

1 cup sugar

1 cup all-purpose flour

1 teaspoon baking powder

½ teaspoon salt

1 teaspoon vanilla extract

2 egg whites

1 Melt butter in a 10-inch cast-iron skillet over low heat. Sprinkle brown sugar in skillet. Remove from heat.

2 Drain pineapple, reserving ¼ cup juice. Set juice aside. Arrange 7 pineapple slices over sugar mixture. Cut remaining pineapple slices in half; line sides of pan, keeping cut sides up. Place a cherry in the center of each whole pineapple slice; arrange pecan halves between slices in a spoke fashion.

3 Beat 3 egg yolks on high speed of an electric mixer until thick and lemon-colored; gradually add 1 cup sugar, beating well. Combine flour, baking powder, and salt; stir well. Add to egg mixture alternately with reserved pineapple juice, mixing well. Stir in vanilla.

4 Beat egg whites on high speed of an electric mixer until stiff peaks form; fold beaten egg whites into batter. Spoon batter evenly over pineapple in skillet. Bake at 350° for 45–50 minutes, or until cake is set. Let cool for 5 minutes. Invert warm cake onto a serving plate.

STRAWBERRY PATCH SHORTCAKE

March to May is peak strawberry time in the South. This is by far the most popular Southern strawberry dessert—nothing tastes better than a mouthful of shortcake, fresh juicy berries, and luscious whipped cream.

YIELD: 8 SERVINGS

INGREDIENTS

1 quart fresh strawberries, sliced
¼ cup sugar
2 cups all-purpose flour
¼ cup sugar
1 tablespoon baking powder
½ teaspoon salt
⅓ cup unsalted butter
¾ cup milk
1 egg
1 egg white
2 tablespoons sugar
1 cup whipping cream
3 tablespoons sifted powdered sugar

1 Combine sliced strawberries and ¼ cup sugar; stir gently. Cover and refrigerate for 2 hours.

2 Lightly grease two 9-inch cake pans; set aside. Combine flour, ¼ cup sugar, baking powder, and salt in a large mixing bowl; cut in butter with a pastry blender until mixture resembles coarse meal. Combine milk and egg; beat well. Add to flour mixture, stirring with a fork until a soft dough forms. Pat dough out evenly into cake pans (dough will be sticky, so moisten fingers with water).

3 Beat egg white until stiff peaks form. Brush surface of dough in each cake pan with egg white. Sprinkle each layer with a tablespoon of sugar. Bake at 450° for 8–10 minutes or until golden brown. Remove shortcakes from pans and let cool completely on wire racks (layers will be thin).

4 Beat whipping cream on high speed of an electric mixer until foamy; gradually add 3 tablespoons powdered sugar, beating until soft peaks form. Place 1 shortcake on a serving plate. Spread half of whipped cream over layer and arrange half of sliced strawberries on top, using a slotted spoon. Repeat procedure with remaining shortcake layer, whipped cream (reserve a little for the decoration), and sliced strawberries. Decorate top of shortcake with the reserved whipped cream.

LOW COUNTRY SHERRY TRIFLE

Trifle portrays the elegance and rich style of Charleston and Savannah, especially when served in a stately trifle bowl. This luscious version is made with pound cake, sherry-flavored custard, and whipped cream.

YIELD: 12 SERVINGS

INGREDIENTS
6 cups milk
1½ cups sugar
2 tablespoons cornstarch
6 eggs
½ cup cream sherry
1½ pounds sliced pound cake
2 cups whipping cream, whipped
maraschino cherries

1 Heat milk in top of a double boiler until steaming, but not boiling.

2 Combine sugar and cornstarch, stirring well. Stir in eggs; beat on low speed of an electric blender until thick and lemon colored. Stir a small amount of hot milk into egg mixture; add to remaining hot milk in double boiler. Cook, stirring constantly, until custard thickens and coats a metal spoon. Cool completely. Stir sherry into custard.

3 Place half of pound cake evenly in bottom of a 5-quart trifle or clear glass bowl. Pour half of custard mixture over pound cake. Spread half of whipped cream over custard. Repeat layers. Garnish with cherries.

HUMMINGBIRD CAKE

In 1978, *Southern Living* magazine printed this recipe from a North Carolina reader, and suddenly the cake was all the rage among Southern cooks. The name is probably due to the fact that the cake is sweet as nectar.

YIELD: ONE 3–LAYER CAKE

INGREDIENTS

3 cups all-purpose flour
2 cups sugar
1 teaspoon baking soda
1 teaspoon salt
1 teaspoon ground cinnamon
3 eggs, beaten
1 cup vegetable oil
1½ teaspoons vanilla extract
1 (8-ounce) can crushed
pineapple, undrained
1 cup chopped pecans
2 cups chopped bananas
½ cup chopped pecans,
lightly toasted

Cream Cheese Frosting
(Yield: about 3½ cups)
1 (8-ounce) package cream
cheese, softened
½ cup butter or margarine,
softened
1 (16-ounce) package
powdered sugar
1 teaspoon vanilla extract

1 Combine first 5 ingredients in a large mixing bowl; add eggs and oil, stirring until dry ingredients are moistened. Add the vanilla, pineapple, 1 cup pecans, and bananas.

2 Spoon batter into 3 greased and floured 9-inch round cake pans. Bake at 350° for 25–30 minutes or until a wooden pick inserted in center comes out clean. Cool cake in pans for 10 minutes; remove from pans, and cool completely.

3 Combine cream cheese and butter, beat on medium speed of an electric mixer until smooth. Add powdered sugar and vanilla; beat until light and fluffy.

4 Spread frosting between layers and on top and sides of cake; sprinkle ½ cup pecans on top.

CHOCOLATE ROULADE

This impressive dessert is easy to make. Don't worry if it cracks a bit when rolled up; just sprinkle on extra sugar. It will look beautiful and taste great!

YIELD: 8 SERVINGS

INGREDIENTS

5 eggs, separated
1 cup sugar
6 tablespoons sifted cocoa
1 cup sifted cake flour
1 teaspoon unflavored gelatin
2 tablespoons cold water
1¼ cups whipping cream
3 tablespoons powdered sugar
½ teaspoon vanilla extract
powdered sugar, for sprinkling

Raspberry Coulis

2 cups raspberries
2 tablespoons powdered sugar

1 Grease the bottom and sides of a 15- x 10- x 1-inch jelly-roll pan with vegetable oil and line with wax paper; grease and flour wax paper. Set pan aside.

2 Place egg yolks in a large bowl and beat on high speed of an electric mixer until foamy. Gradually add 1 cup sugar, beating until thick and lemon-colored. Gradually stir in 3 tablespoons cocoa.

3 Beat egg whites until stiff peaks form; fold into cocoa mixture. Gently fold cake flour into egg mixture. Spread batter evenly in prepared pan. Bake at 350° for 15 minutes.

4 Sift remaining cocoa onto a dish towel in a 15- x 10- inch rectangle. When cake is done, loosen from sides of pan and gently, but quickly, turn cake out onto towel. Peel off wax paper. Beginning at narrow end, roll up cake and towel; place seam side down on a wire rack and let cool.

5 Sprinkle gelatin over 2 tablespoons cold water in a small saucepan; let stand for 1 minute. Cook over low heat, stirring until gelatin dissolves. Beat whipping cream on low speed of an electric mixer, gradually adding dissolved gelatin mixture. Increase to medium speed and continue to beat until mixture begins to thicken. Add powdered sugar and vanilla; beat at high speed until soft peaks form.

6 To make the raspberry coulis, put the raspberries and sugar into a food processor and process to a smooth puree. Press through a strainer to remove the seeds.

7 Unroll cake and remove towel. Spread whipped cream mixture on cake, leaving a 1-inch margin around edges; reroll cake. Place on serving plate, seam side down. Sprinkle the roulade with **powdered** sugar, and serve in slices with the raspberry coulis poured over.

MINT JULEPS

The powerful taste of a mint julep can be surprising. If you expect a dainty concoction, it will only take one sip to put those thoughts to rest. Mint juleps are traditionally served in frosty silver mint julep cups.

YIELD: 24 SERVINGS

INGREDIENTS

1 cup lightly packed fresh
mint sprigs

1½ cups water

1 cup sugar

1½ gallons crushed ice

1½ quarts bourbon

sprigs of fresh mint

1 Place 1 cup lightly packed mint sprigs in a heavy saucepan; crush mint with fingers or bruise with the back of a spoon. Add 1½ cups water to saucepan; bring mixture to a boil. Cook, covered, for 5 minutes. Add sugar, stirring well; return to a boil. Cover, reduce heat, and simmer for 5 minutes. Let syrup cool. Place mint syrup in a small bowl or jar; cover and let stand for 4–6 hours. Strain mixture, discarding mint and reserving syrup.

2 To serve, fill each julep cup or small glass with 1 cup crushed ice. Add 1 tablespoon syrup mixture and ¼ cup bourbon for each serving, stirring gently. Garnish with sprigs of fresh mint.

Did you know?

If you put a few stalks of freshly picked mint in a jar of water, within a few days they will grow roots, which can be planted indoors for a year-round supply.

CHAMPAGNE PUNCH

When entertaining the ladies, this is a punch that has proven popular. It is a refreshing blend of citrus juice and champagne; add a little grenadine or cherry juice for a pretty pink color.

**YIELD: ABOUT
3½ QUARTS**

INGREDIENTS

2 (6-ounce) cans frozen orange juice concentrate, thawed and undiluted

2 (6-ounce) cans frozen lemonade concentrate, thawed and undiluted

1 (1-quart) bottle tonic water

ice cubes or ice ring

1 (1-quart) bottle ginger ale, chilled

1 (750-milliliter) bottle champagne or sparkling wine, chilled

½ cup grenadine or maraschino cherry juice (optional)

1 Combine orange juice concentrate, lemonade concentrate, and tonic water; refrigerate until chilled. Pour mixture over ice in a large punch bowl. Gently stir in ginger ale and champagne. Add grenadine or cherry juice if a pink color is desired.

Recipes

Summer

OKRA PICKLES

If you have never tried okra pickles, you will be surprised, for they are crisp and flavorful and make a delightful appetizer.

YIELD: 7 PINTS

INGREDIENTS

3½ pounds small okra pods

14 cloves garlic

7 small fresh red or green chili peppers

1 quart water

1 pint white vinegar (5% acidity)

⅓ cup pickling salt

1 tablespoon dill seeds

1 Wash okra thoroughly. Pack okra tightly into 7 hot sterilized pint jars; place 2 garlic cloves and a hot pepper in each jar. Combine 1 quart water, the vinegar, pickling salt, and dill seeds in a saucepan; bring to a boil.

2 Pour boiling vinegar mixture over okra, leaving ½-inch headspace. Remove air bubbles; wipe jar rims. Cover at once with metal lids and screw on bands. Process in boiling-water bath for 10 minutes.

3 Alternatively, transfer the pickles into a sterilized clip-lock jar. Pour the vinegar into the jars to cover the pickles and seal while hot. Let cool and store in the refrigerator for 2 weeks before using, and use within two months.

CRISP SWEET PICKLES

Soaking in pickling lime makes these pickles so crisp that they seem to snap when you bite into them. The lime can be purchased at most grocery stores during summer months.

YIELD: ABOUT 8 PINTS

INGREDIENTS

7 pounds small cucumbers
2 gallons water
2 cups pickling lime
2 quarts crushed ice
8 cups white vinegar
(5% acidity)
8 cups sugar
1 tablespoon salt
2 teaspoons mixed pickling
spices

1 Wash cucumbers and slice into ¼-inch-thick slices. Combine cucumber slices, 2 gallons water, and pickling lime in a large crockery bowl; let soak for 12 hours. Drain cucumber slices and rinse in cold water; repeat draining and rinsing procedure three times (to remove lime). Pack crushed ice over cucumbers; cover and let stand for 4 hours. Drain well.

2 Heat vinegar, sugar, salt, and pickling spices in a large saucepan, stirring constantly, until mixture comes to a boil and sugar dissolves. Pour syrup mixture over cucumbers; let stand for 5–6 hours or overnight.

3 Bring cucumber-and-syrup mixture to a boil; reduce heat, and simmer for 35 minutes. Pack into hot sterilized jars, leaving ½-inch headspace. Remove air bubbles; wipe jar rims. Cover at once with metal lids and screw on bands. Process in boiling-water bath for 10 minutes. See page 66 for alternative storage in a sterilized clip-lock jar.

YELLOW SQUASH PICKLES

Faced with the dilemma of excess bounty, gardeners often turn to canning in order to set some of the vegetables aside for winter months. This bright yellow pickle is one of the best ways to enjoy summer squash all year long.

YIELD: 7 PINTS

INGREDIENTS

16 cups sliced small yellow squash

1½ large onions, sliced

1 small red bell pepper, chopped

¾ cup salt

3¾ cups sugar

2¼ cups white vinegar (5% acidity)

¼ cup pickling salt

2 teaspoons celery seeds

2 teaspoons mustard seeds

2 teaspoons ground turmeric

1 Combine squash, onion, and red bell pepper in a large bowl; sprinkle with the salt. Cover and let stand for 2 hours. Rinse vegetables several times in cold water; drain well.

2 Combine remaining ingredients in a medium saucepan; bring to a boil. Cook, stirring constantly, until sugar dissolves.

3 Pack vegetables into hot sterilized jars; cover with hot vinegar mixture, leaving ½-inch headspace. Remove air bubbles; wipe jar rims. Cover at once with metal lids and screw on bands. Process in boiling-water bath for 15 minutes. See page 66 for alternative storage in a sterilized clip-lock jar.

FAVORITE FIG PRESERVES

Figs are grown in backyards all over the South. It's fun to eat fresh figs with vanilla ice cream or to toss them into salads, but this fruit is at its best cooked into syrupy preserves and spread over a hot biscuit or roll.

YIELD: 5 PINTS

INGREDIENTS
5 quarts ripe fresh figs
5 cups sugar

1 Wash figs several times, removing and discarding stems. Place figs in a large Dutch oven or kettle. Cover with sugar; let stand overnight (liquid will drain from figs).

2 Cook fig mixture over low heat for 2 to 3 hours (cooking time will vary according to ripeness of figs), stirring occasionally, until most of the liquid has evaporated and mixture thickens (some figs will fall apart).

3 Spoon figs into hot sterilized jars, leaving ¼-inch headspace. Remove air bubbles; wipe jar rims. Cover at once with metal lids and screw on bands. Process in boiling-water bath for 10 minutes. See page 66 for alternative storage in a sterilized clip-lock jar.

HOT PEPPER JELLY

Sweet-hot pepper jelly makes a mouthwatering appetizer when spooned over cream cheese and spread over crackers. If desired, the jelly can be tinted red or green and shared with friends as a holiday gift.

YIELD: 6 HALF PINTS OR 12 QUARTER PINTS

INGREDIENTS

1¼ cups minced green bell pepper

½ cup minced hot green chili pepper

7¼ cups sugar

1½ cups cider vinegar (5% acidity)

2 (3-ounce) packages liquid pectin

green or red food coloring (optional)

1 Combine peppers, sugar, and vinegar in a Dutch oven; bring to a boil. Boil for 5 minutes, stirring frequently. Add pectin and several drops of food coloring, if desired. Bring mixture to a full rolling boil; boil for 1 minute, stirring frequently. Remove from heat and skim off foam with a metal spoon.

2 Quickly pour hot jelly into hot sterilized jars, leaving ¼-inch headspace; wipe jar rims. Cover at once with metal lids and screw on bands. Process in boiling-water bath for 5 minutes. See page 66 for alternative storage in a sterilized clip-lock jar.

Bell peppers are native to South America and date back about 5,000 years. They were introduced to Europe in the Middle Ages by Spanish and Portugese explorers.

SHRIMP WITH COCKTAIL SAUCE

Two tips for perfectly cooked shrimp: Add to simmering, but not boiling water, and rinse with cold water as soon as they turn opaque. Leaving the shells on will give the shrimp a rich pink color.

YIELD: 6 SERVINGS

INGREDIENTS
2 quarts water
1 (3-ounce) package crab and shrimp boil
1 tablespoon salt
1 tablespoon cayenne pepper
2 bay leaves
2½ pounds unpeeled fresh shrimp

**Cocktail Sauce
(Yield: 1⅓ cups)**
1¼ cups chili sauce
3 tablespoons lemon juice
3 tablespoons prepared horseradish
2 teaspoons Worcestershire sauce
3 dashes hot sauce

1 To make the cocktail sauce, combine all ingredients, stirring until smooth. Cover and refrigerate for at least 1 hour.

2 Combine 2 quarts water, crab and shrimp boil, salt, cayenne, and bay leaves in a large stockpot; bring to a boil. Reduce heat, and gently simmer for 10 minutes. Add shrimp; cook for 3–5 minutes, or just until shrimp turn pink. Drain well; rinse with cold water. Refrigerate until chilled. Peel and devein shrimp. Serve with cocktail sauce.

FRIED OKRA

You won't be able to resist tasty little morsels of fried okra. The pods are sliced, dredged in cornmeal and flour, and fried until crisp and crunchy. It makes a great appetizer or side dish.

YIELD: 6–8 SERVINGS

INGREDIENTS
1½ pounds fresh okra
2 eggs, beaten
⅓ cup buttermilk
1 cup all-purpose flour
1 cup cornmeal
½ teaspoon salt
vegetable oil for frying

1 Wash okra and cut into ¾-inch slices; pat dry with paper towels. Combine eggs and buttermilk in a large bowl; stir well. Add okra and let soak for 10 minutes. Drain.

2 Combine flour, cornmeal, and salt in a medium bowl. Dredge okra, a few pieces at a time, in flour mixture, coating well.

3 Heat vegetable oil to 375°. Fry okra in hot oil until golden. Drain on paper towels.

REFRIGERATOR CORN RELISH

This easy summer relish is tasty enough to be served as a vegetable side dish, but it can also double as a condiment to accompany your favorite grilled fish, chicken, or steak.

YIELD: 4–6 SERVINGS

INGREDIENTS

½ cup water

2 cups fresh corn cut from cob (about 4 ears)

4 green onions, thinly sliced

2 large tomatoes, diced

1 medium green bell pepper, diced

⅛ cup vegetable oil

⅛ cup vinegar

1 tablespoon sugar

2 teaspoons minced fresh basil

2 teaspoons minced fresh parsley

½ teaspoon crushed red pepper flakes

1 Place water in a small saucepan and bring to a boil; add corn kernels. Cover, reduce heat and simmer for 10 minutes or just until kernels are crisp-tender. Drain; rinse with cold water and drain again.

2 Combine corn kernels, onions, tomatoes, and bell pepper, stirring well.

3 Combine oil, vinegar, sugar, basil, parsley, and red pepper flakes, stirring well. Pour over corn mixture. Cover and refrigerate for several hours or until chilled.

DEVILED EGGS

The yolks of these hard-cooked eggs are removed, mashed, and combined with pickles, olives, vinegar, and mustard. Spoon the spicy mixture back into the whites for stuffed eggs just right for serving on picnics or at luncheons.

YIELD: 6 SERVINGS

INGREDIENTS

6 hard-cooked eggs, peeled
¼ cup mayonnaise
2 tablespoons chopped sweet pickles
1 tablespoon chopped green olives
1 teaspoon cider vinegar
1 teaspoon prepared mustard
¼ teaspoon salt
¼ teaspoon black pepper
paprika

1 Slice eggs in half lengthwise, and carefully remove yolks. Mash yolks with mayonnaise in a bowl. Add remaining ingredients except paprika and stir well. Spoon yolk mixture into egg whites. Sprinkle stuffed eggs with paprika.

76

FRIED GREEN TOMATOES

Fried green tomatoes are the perfect use for late summer tomatoes that refuse to ripen. It seems all Southerners are entranced with this cornmeal-crusted treat.

YIELD: 6 SERVINGS

INGREDIENTS

1 cup cornmeal
2 teaspoons brown sugar
½ teaspoon salt
⅛ teaspoon black pepper
3 large green tomatoes, sliced
1 egg, beaten
vegetable oil, for frying

1 Combine cornmeal, sugar, salt, and pepper in a small bowl; stir well. Dip tomato slices in beaten egg; dredge in cornmeal mixture, coating well on both sides.

2 Heat 2–3 tablespoons oil in a large cast-iron skillet over medium-high heat until hot. Add a layer of tomatoes; fry for 3–5 minutes or until browned, turning once. Remove slices and drain. Repeat procedure, adding more oil to pan as needed, until all slices have been fried. Serve immediately.

MARINATED TOMATOES & CUCUMBERS

Tomatoes and cucumbers are perfectly partnered in this tangy vinegar and dill weed dressing. The salad can be made ahead and stored in the refrigerator, which makes it ideal for serving on hot summer evenings.

YIELD: 6 SERVINGS

INGREDIENTS

3 large tomatoes, sliced
1 large cucumber, thinly sliced
½ cup cider vinegar
½ cup vegetable oil
1 teaspoon sugar
1 teaspoon dried dill weed
½ teaspoon salt
½ teaspoon black pepper
lettuce leaves

1 Place tomato slices and cucumber slices in a large shallow container. Combine vinegar, oil, sugar, dill weed, salt, and pepper; stir well and pour over vegetables. Cover and refrigerate for at least 2 hours. Just before serving, remove tomatoes and cucumbers with a slotted spoon, and arrange on lettuce leaves. Drizzle with remaining marinade, if desired.

FRIED ONION RINGS

You wouldn't want to eat fried onion rings at every meal, but they certainly are good served with fish or hamburgers. The buttermilk batter, made fluffy with beaten egg whites, creates an extra-light, golden coating.

YIELD: 4–6 SERVINGS

INGREDIENTS

2 large Spanish or Vidalia onions
2¼ cups all-purpose flour
1 tablespoon cornmeal
1½ teaspoons baking powder
1 teaspoon salt
2 cups buttermilk
2 eggs, separated
vegetable oil
chili sauce

1 Peel onions; cut into ½-inch-thick slices, and separate into rings. Place rings in a large bowl of ice water. Let stand for 30 minutes; drain on paper towels.

2 Place drained onion rings in a large plastic or paper bag; add 1 cup flour, and shake until rings are coated.

3 Combine remaining 1¼ cups flour, cornmeal, baking powder, salt, and buttermilk; stir in egg yolks, mixing well. Beat egg whites until stiff peaks form; fold into batter.

4 Dip onion rings in batter, coating well. Heat oil (1 to 2 inches) in a Dutch oven or large, deep skillet to 375°, and fry the onion rings, a few at a time, for 3-5 minutes, or until golden brown. Drain on paper towels. Serve immediately with chili sauce for dipping.

Tips
Stored in an airy, dry, and cool place without touching each other, most onions will last for several months, although the vitamin C content will diminish over time.

POTATO SALAD

No picnic is complete without a bowl of potato salad. Use Russet or waxy red potatoes because they contain less starch than baking potatoes and will not crumble when ingredients are tossed together.

YIELD: 6–8 SERVINGS

INGREDIENTS

8 large Russet or red potatoes, peeled and cubed
2 hard-cooked eggs, chopped
½ cup chopped celery
½ cup sweet pickle relish
¼ cup chopped green onions
1 (2-ounce) jar diced pimiento, drained
½ cup mayonnaise
½ cup sour cream
1 teaspoon prepared mustard
½ teaspoon salt
¼ teaspoon black pepper

1 Cook potatoes in boiling salted water to cover for 20 minutes, or until tender. Drain and cool slightly. Combine potatoes, eggs, celery, pickle relish, onions, and pimiento in a large bowl, tossing gently.

2 Combine mayonnaise, sour cream, mustard, salt, and pepper, stirring well; add to vegetable mixture, tossing gently.

COUNTRY COLESLAW

Fried fish and hush puppies go hand in hand with creamy coleslaw. A small amount of shredded red cabbage can be stirred in for brighter color.

YIELD: 10 SERVINGS

INGREDIENTS

1 small cabbage, shredded

1½ cups shredded carrots

½ cup diced green bell pepper

½ cup sweet pickle relish

¾–1 cup mayonnaise

1 tablespoon sugar

½ teaspoon salt

Tips

Keep cabbage stored in the refrigerator in a plastic bag to retain its vitamin C and freshness.

If using a red cabbage to enhance the color of your coleslaw, remember to sprinkle the cabbage with lemon juice to prevent it turning a not-so-appetizing gray!

1 Combine cabbage, carrots, green pepper, and pickle relish in a large bowl; toss gently to combine.

2 Combine mayonnaise, sugar, and salt; stir well. Pour mixture over cabbage, tossing gently to combine. Cover and refrigerate for at least 30 minutes, or until serving time.

BAKED BEANS

This simple baked beans recipe is a great choice to take to covered-dish dinners, and it is an absolute must whenever you plan a fish fry or barbecue.

YIELD: 6 SERVINGS

INGREDIENTS

2 (16-ounce) cans pork and beans
¾ cup firmly packed brown sugar
½ cup chopped onion
½ cup catsup
¼ cup chopped green bell pepper
2 teaspoons prepared mustard
4 slices bacon
1 green bell pepper,
cut into thin rings

1 Combine all ingredients, except bacon and pepper rings; stir well. Spoon into a lightly greased 2-quart baking dish. Arrange bacon slices and pepper rings over top. Bake at 350°, uncovered, for 1 hour.

SWEET CORN CUSTARD

Fresh corn is one of the sweetest joys of summer. When cutting corn from the cob, use this rule of thumb: Two average-size ears of corn will yield about one cup of kernels.

YIELD: 6–8 SERVINGS

INGREDIENTS

2 cups fresh corn cut from cob (about 4 ears)

3 eggs, beaten

¾ cup (3 ounces) shredded cheddar cheese

¼ cup all-purpose flour

4 teaspoons sugar

½ teaspoon salt

⅛ teaspoon black pepper

⅛ teaspoon ground nutmeg

2 cups half-and-half

2 tablespoons unsalted butter or margarine, melted

1 Combine corn, eggs, and cheese in a large bowl, stirring well.

2 Combine flour, sugar, salt, pepper, and nutmeg; add to corn mixture. Stir in half-and-half and butter. Pour mixture into a lightly greased 1½-quart shallow baking dish. Place the dish in a 13- x 9- x 2-inch pan; add hot water to baking pan to a depth of 1 inch up sides of pan.

3 Bake at 350°, uncovered, for 1 hour, or until a knife inserted in center comes out clean.

TANGY GREEN BEANS WITH BACON

There was a time when cooks simmered green beans for hours, usually with a piece of bacon or ham hock. But modern cooks have come to value the fresher flavor and more defined texture of beans that simmer for a shorter time.

YIELD: 4-6 SERVINGS

INGREDIENTS

1¼ pounds fresh green beans
4 slices bacon
1 small onion, chopped
¾ cup sugar
½ cup cider vinegar

1 Remove strings from beans; wash beans and cut into 1-inch pieces. Set aside.

2 Cook bacon in a large skillet over medium-high heat until crisp; remove bacon, reserving drippings. Crumble bacon and set aside.

3 Sauté onion in bacon drippings until tender. Add sugar, stirring until dissolved. Stir in bacon, beans, and vinegar. Cover and bring to a boil, reduce heat, and simmer for 20 minutes, or just until beans are tender.

GREEN BEAN & NEW POTATO SALAD

Green beans, new potatoes, and cherry tomatoes are often grown in backyard gardens. Enjoy their fresh flavors tossed together in a salad dressed with tangy vinaigrette.

YIELD: 4–6 SERVINGS

INGREDIENTS

½ pound new potatoes, peeled and cubed

1 pound fresh green beans

10 cherry tomatoes, halved

¼ cup olive oil

2 tablespoons white wine vinegar

2 tablespoons lemon juice

1 tablespoon finely chopped fresh basil or 1 teaspoon dried basil

½ teaspoon salt

¼ teaspoon garlic powder

¼ teaspoon coarsely ground black pepper

1 Cook potatoes in enough boiling water to cover for 15 minutes, or until just tender. Drain, and set aside.

2 Remove strings from beans. Cut beans into 1½-inch pieces. Wash thoroughly. Cover beans with water and bring to a boil. Reduce heat, cover, and simmer 8 to 10 minutes or until crisp-tender. Drain.

3 Combine potatoes, beans, and tomatoes in a large bowl, tossing gently. Combine remaining ingredients in a small bowl, stirring vigorously; pour dressing over vegetables and toss gently. Cover and refrigerate for at least 4 hours.

Local Beans $3.75 qt.

Green beans are the unripe fruit of any bean plant. There are three main types: French (stringless) beans, runner (string) beans, and snap beans.

Tips
Buy beans loose from a market where possible, so that you can select those with a smooth feel, bright green color, and a pleasing snap when broken in half.

BUTTER BEAN SALAD

During summer months Southern cooks shell pale green butter beans or baby limas to enjoy simmered with ham hock or salt pork. A cold salad, such as the one below, can be created from the leftover cooked beans.

YIELD: 4–6 SERVINGS

INGREDIENTS

4 cups cooked butter beans, drained

½ cup chopped celery

2 green onions, chopped

2 hard-cooked eggs, coarsely chopped

¼ cup chopped green bell pepper

1 (2-ounce) jar diced pimiento, drained

2 tablespoons chopped fresh parsley

½ cup mayonnaise

lettuce leaves

1 Combine beans, celery, onions, eggs, green pepper, pimiento, and parsley, tossing gently. Stir in mayonnaise. Cover and refrigerate for at least several hours.

2 Serve salad over lettuce leaves.

CORNBREAD SALAD

It was a creative cook who first turned cornbread into this colorful salad. Cut leftover or freshly baked cornbread into cubes, then toss with tomatoes, bell pepper, red onion, celery, and pecans.

YIELD: 6–8 SERVINGS

INGREDIENTS

1 (8-inch) square baked cornbread, cooled

2 large tomatoes, diced

1 large green bell pepper, finely chopped

½ cup chopped pecans, toasted

⅓ cup chopped red onion

2 stalks celery, finely chopped

1 (4-ounce) jar diced pimiento, drained

½ teaspoon salt

¼ teaspoon black pepper

⅔ cup mayonnaise

1 Cut cooled cornbread into ¾-inch cubes. Spread cornbread cubes on a baking sheet; bake at 250° for 30 minutes. Let cool.

2 Combine diced tomato, green pepper, pecans, onion, celery, pimiento, salt, and black pepper in a large bowl, tossing gently. Stir in cornbread cubes and mayonnaise. Cover and refrigerate for at least 30 minutes before serving.

HUSH PUPPIES

Hush puppies were created in the fishing camps along the coast of north Florida. While camp cooks were frying fish, they would throw scraps of fried batter to barking dogs and yell, "Hush, puppies!"

YIELD: ABOUT 1½ DOZEN

INGREDIENTS

1 cup cornmeal
½ cup all-purpose flour
1½ teaspoons baking powder
1 teaspoon salt
1 teaspoon sugar
¼ teaspoon garlic powder
¼ teaspoon black pepper
⅛ teaspoon cayenne pepper
1 egg, beaten
⅔ cup milk
⅓ cup minced onion
vegetable oil

1 Combine cornmeal, flour, baking powder, salt, sugar, garlic powder, black pepper, and cayenne pepper in a large bowl. Add egg, milk, and onion, stirring just until dry ingredients are moistened. Let batter stand for 3–5 minutes.

2 Drop batter by rounded tablespoonfuls into hot oil (375°) in a large, deep skillet. Cook, turning once, for 3–5 minutes, or until hush puppies float to top of oil and are golden brown. Drain well on paper towels.

Hush Puppies are often paired with delicious Delta Fried Catfish (see page 100), traditionally these golden cornbread dumplings were cooked in the same pan that the catfish were fried in, using the same fat for extra flavor.

SUMMER TUNA SALAD

This creamy congealed mixture can be served as a salad for lunch. It also makes a wonderful appetizer spread over crackers.

YIELD: 6 SERVINGS

INGREDIENTS

1 envelope unflavored gelatin

1 cup cold water

4 hard-cooked eggs, chopped

1 (8½-ounce) can English peas, drained

1 (6½-ounce) can tuna packed in water, drained and flaked

1 medium green pepper, chopped

¾ cup celery, finely chopped

1 cup mayonnaise

½ cup pickle relish

2 tablespoons lemon juice

lettuce leaves

1 Sprinkle gelatin over cold water in a saucepan; let stand for 1 minute. Cook over low heat, stirring until gelatin dissolves.

2 Combine eggs, peas, tuna, green pepper, celery, mayonnaise, pickle relish, and lemon juice; stir in gelatin mixture. Pour into a lightly oiled 6-cup mold; cover and refrigerate until firm. Unmold salad on lettuce leaves.

BLUE CRAB & WILD RICE SALAD

The season for blue crabs runs from April to October. Here the delicately flavored crabmeat is combined into a colorful salad combination that looks elegant served on a bed of lettuce or in a tomato "flower."

YIELD: 6–8 SERVINGS

INGREDIENTS

1 (4-ounce) package wild rice
1 pound fresh blue crabmeat, drained and flaked
1¼ cups frozen tiny English peas, thawed
½ cup chopped green onions
1 (4-ounce) jar diced pimiento, drained
½ cup mayonnaise
½ cup sour cream
1 tablespoon lemon juice
1½ teaspoons curry powder
tomato or lettuce leaves

1 Cook rice according to package directions; let cool. Combine rice, crabmeat, peas, green onions, and pimiento, stirring gently.

2 Combine mayonnaise, sour cream, lemon juice, and curry powder; add to crabmeat mixture, stirring gently. Slice a tomato into wedges, cutting to, but not through the bottom of the tomato; spread tomato wedges and fill with salad, or serve salad over lettuce leaves.

SUMMER SUCCOTASH

While succotash may have originated with the Indians, today it is a favorite Southern side dish, especially when made with garden-fresh lima beans and corn cut from the cob.

YIELD: 4–6 SERVINGS

INGREDIENTS

4 slices bacon

1 medium onion, chopped

¼ cup chopped green bell pepper

2 cups shelled fresh lima beans (about 1 pound)

2 cups fresh corn cut from the cob (about 4 ears)

2 tablespoons butter or margarine

⅛ teaspoon black pepper

1 Cook bacon in a large skillet until crisp; remove bacon and set aside, reserving drippings.

2 Sauté onion and green pepper in bacon drippings until vegetables are tender. Add lima beans, corn, butter, and black pepper; cover and cook over low heat for 30 minutes or until vegetables are tender. Crumble reserved bacon and sprinkle over top.

SUMMER GAZPACHO

This cold soup originated in Spain, but it is perfect for serving on hot evenings when tomatoes are plentiful. The soup can be made ahead and kept in the refrigerator.

YIELD: 10 CUPS

INGREDIENTS

4 cups tomato juice

3 cups peeled, chopped tomatoes

1½ cups tomato purée

1¼ cups water

1 cup peeled, chopped cucumber

¾ cup finely chopped green bell pepper

½ cup finely chopped green onion

⅓ cup Italian salad dressing

2 cloves garlic, minced

3 tablespoons red wine vinegar

1 tablespoon lemon juice

¼ teaspoon salt

¼ teaspoon black pepper

⅛ teaspoon hot sauce

ice cubes

1 Combine all ingredients, except ice cubes, in a large bowl and stir. Cover and refrigerate overnight. Ladle into soup bowls; add a single ice cube and serve.

CHILLED CUCUMBER SOUP

Cold cucumber soup is a refreshing treat on a hot summer day. This soup tastes great, looks pretty, and is the ideal accompaniment to a salad or sandwich.

YIELD: 4 SERVINGS

INGREDIENTS

3 cucumbers, peeled, seeded, and chopped

2 cups sour cream

1 cup half-and-half

1 green onion, chopped

1 tablespoon lemon juice

2 teaspoons minced fresh dill weed or ½ teaspoon dried dill weed

½ teaspoon garlic salt

¼ teaspoon white pepper

1 Combine all ingredients in container of an electric blender; process until smooth. Cover and refrigerate until thoroughly chilled.

DELTA FRIED CATFISH

Numerous celebrations across the South honor the catfish, but the most lavish is the World Catfish Festival in Belzoni, Mississippi; this area produces more farm-raised catfish than any other place in the United States.

YIELD: 6 SERVINGS

INGREDIENTS

6 whole, cleaned catfish
(4–5 pounds)
3 cups cornmeal
1¼ teaspoon salt
2½ cups buttermilk
vegetable oil
lettuce leaves and lemon wedges

1 Rinse fish under cold water; pat dry and set aside.

2 Combine cornmeal and salt in a large bowl. Dip fish in buttermilk and dredge in cornmeal mixture.

3 Heat oil (1 to 2 inches) in a Dutch oven or large, deep skillet to 350°, and fry fish until they float to top and are golden brown. Drain well on paper towels. Serve immediately with lettuce leaves and a lemon wedge.

CRABMEAT AU GRATIN

Fresh blue crabs are a rich reward when caught in crab pots at the end of a pier and cracked and cooked for dinner. The flaky white meat can be stirred into this rich, creamy casserole.

YIELD: 4 SERVINGS

INGREDIENTS

2 tablespoons unsalted butter
or margarine
1 tablespoon all-purpose flour
¼ teaspoon salt
⅛ teaspoon black pepper
1 cup milk
1 teaspoon Worcestershire
sauce
2 egg yolks
1 teaspoon minced green bell
pepper
1 teaspoon minced onion
1 pound fresh blue crabmeat,
drained and flaked
1 tablespoon unsalted butter
or margarine, melted
½ cup soft fresh bread crumbs
¼ cup finely shredded
cheddar cheese
paprika
tomato and basil salad
lemon wedges

1 Melt 2 tablespoons butter in a heavy saucepan over low heat; gradually add flour, salt, and black pepper, stirring until smooth. Cook for 1 minute, stirring constantly. Gradually add milk; cook over medium heat, stirring constantly, until thickened and bubbly. Stir in Worcestershire sauce.

2 Beat egg yolks until thick and lemon colored. Stir some of the hot mixture into yolks; add to remaining hot mixture, stirring constantly. Stir in green pepper, onion, and crabmeat.

3 Spoon crabmeat mixture into individual baking shells or a lightly greased 1½-quart shallow baking dish. Bake at 350° for 20 minutes. Combine 1 tablespoon melted butter, bread crumbs, and cheese; sprinkle over casserole. Bake for 5 minutes or until cheese melts and mixture is hot and bubbly. Sprinkle with paprika. Serve gratin with a tomato and basil salad a lemon wedge.

There are more than 8,000 species of fresh and saltwater crabs.

Every year, over 1 million tons are eaten.

SIMPLE STUFFED SQUASH

Mild-flavored yellow squash is delicious stewed, steamed, fried, or baked. This recipe always impresses dinner guests because it looks pretty on the plate; the squash are cooked whole, then cut in half and stuffed.

YIELD: 6 SERVINGS

INGREDIENTS

6 medium-size yellow squash

6 slices bacon

1 medium onion, chopped

1 tablespoon minced green bell pepper

½ cup chicken broth

1 cup fine dry bread crumbs

½ teaspoon salt

½ teaspoon black pepper

¼ cup unsalted butter or margarine, melted

parmesan cheese

Don't throw away nutritious squash seeds —they can be dried in an oven on a low heat and eaten in the same way as pumpkin seeds.

1 Wash squash thoroughly. Place squash in a large saucepan; add enough water to cover. Bring water to a boil; cover, reduce heat, and simmer for 10–15 minutes, or until squash is tender but still firm. Drain and cool slightly. Trim off stems. Cut squash in half lengthwise; remove and reserve pulp, leaving a firm shell. Set aside.

2 Fry bacon over medium heat until crisp. Remove bacon, reserving 2 tablespoons drippings in skillet.

Crumble bacon and set aside. Sauté onion and green pepper in drippings until tender.

3 Combine onion and green pepper with broth, bacon, bread crumbs, salt, pepper, and squash pulp; mix well. Place the squash shells in a lightly greased 13- x 9- x 2-inch baking dish. Spoon pulp mixture into shells; drizzle with butter and sprinkle with cheese. Bake, uncovered, at 400° for 10 minutes, or until lightly browned.

EGGPLANT CASSEROLE

The purple-black eggplant has gained in popularity because it is prolific in most summer gardens. The mild, almost bland-flavored flesh absorbs the homey flavor of bacon in this easy casserole.

YIELD: 4 SERVINGS

INGREDIENTS

1 large eggplant
4 slices bacon
1 small onion, chopped
1 egg, lightly beaten
1 cup soft or fresh bread crumbs
½ teaspoon salt
⅛ teaspoon black pepper

1 Peel eggplant, and cut into ½-inch cubes. Combine eggplant and water to cover in a saucepan; bring to a boil. Reduce heat, cover, and simmer for 20 minutes. Drain well; cool slightly, and mash eggplant.

2 Cook bacon in a medium skillet over low heat until crisp. Remove bacon, reserving drippings. Crumble bacon and set aside. Sauté onion in drippings until tender.

3 Combine mashed eggplant, bacon, onion, egg, bread crumbs, salt, and pepper, stirring gently. Spoon mixture into a lightly greased 1-quart casserole dish. Bake at 350° for 1 hour.

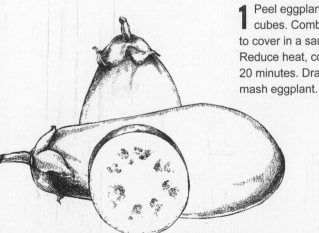

KEY LIME PIE

Authentic Key lime pie uses lime juice from tiny, round Key limes and sweetened condensed milk. Natives insist the pie never be colored with green food coloring, but left a natural pale yellow.

YIELD: 6–8 SERVINGS

INGREDIENTS

Single-Crust Pie Pastry
(*page 152), unbaked
4 egg yolks
½ cup Key lime juice
1 (14-ounce) can sweetened
condensed milk
2 cups whipping cream
¼ cup sifted powdered sugar

1 Line a 9-inch pie plate with pastry; trim and flute edges. Bake at 450° for 12–14 minutes, or until golden brown. Let cool completely.

2 Beat egg yolks with an electric mixer on medium speed until thick and lemon-colored. Heat juice in a saucepan over medium heat until thoroughly heated (about 160° on a candy thermometer). Gradually stir about one-fourth of hot lime juice into yolks; add yolks to remaining hot lime juice in saucepan, stirring constantly. Cook for 2 minutes, stirring constantly.

3 Remove from heat and let cool. Add sweetened condensed milk, stirring until mixture becomes thick. Spoon filling into pie pastry, spreading evenly. Refrigerate until thoroughly chilled.

4 Beat cream on high speed of an electric mixer until foamy. Gradually add sugar, 1 tablespoon at a time, beating until stiff peaks form. Spoon whipped cream onto chilled pie. Refrigerate until serving time.

LEMON ANGEL FOOD CAKE

Some say this light, airy sponge-type cake originated in India. But many Southerners prefer to believe that a frugal ancestor created the cake in order to avoid discarding egg whites left over from other baking projects.

YIELD: ONE 10-INCH CAKE

INGREDIENTS

12 egg whites

1¼ teaspoons cream of tartar

pinch of salt

1½ cups sugar

1 cup sifted cake flour

1 teaspoon lemon extract

½ teaspoon vanilla extract

1 Beat egg whites on high speed of an electric mixer until foamy. Add cream of tartar and salt; beat until soft peaks form. Add sugar, 2 tablespoons at a time, beating until stiff peaks form. Sprinkle flour over egg-white mixture, ¼ cup at a time, folding in carefully each time. Fold in flavorings.

2 Pour batter into an ungreased 10-inch tube pan, spreading evenly. Bake at 350° for 35–45 minutes, or until cake springs back when lightly touched. Remove cake from oven and immediately invert pan; let cool for at least 1 hour. Remove cake from pan.

SUMMER PEACH COBBLER

There are many different recipes for cobbler, but this simple combination of peaches flavored with vanilla and cinnamon and topped with a lattice pastry is destined to be a favorite.

YIELD: 6–8 SERVINGS

INGREDIENTS

1½ cups all-purpose flour
½ teaspoon salt
½ cup solid vegetable shortening
2–4 tablespoons cold water
7½–8 cups sliced fresh peaches
1½ cups sugar
¼ cup all-purpose flour
1½ teaspoons vanilla extract
½ teaspoon ground cinnamon
¼ cup unsalted butter or margarine, melted

1 Combine 1½ cups flour and salt; cut in shortening with a pastry blender until mixture resembles coarse meal. Sprinkle 2–4 tablespoons cold water, a tablespoon at a time, evenly over surface, stirring with a fork until all dry ingredients are moistened. Shape into a ball; cover, and refrigerate until chilled.

2 Combine peaches, sugar, ¼ cup flour, vanilla, cinnamon, and butter in a Dutch oven; stir well and set mixture aside until mixture begins to form a syrup. Bring peach mixture to a boil; reduce heat, and cook, uncovered, for 8–12 minutes, or until peaches are tender. Spoon peaches into a lightly greased 11- x 7- x 2-inch baking dish.

3 Roll out chilled dough to ⅛-inch thickness on a lightly floured surface; cut into 1-inch strips and arrange in a lattice design over peaches. Bake at 475° for 15 minutes, or until pastry is golden.

PEACH ICE CREAM

In the days before electric ice cream makers, ice cream had to be hand-churned, but nobody ever dared to complain. Just the thought of juicy peaches swimming in rich vanilla custard cream made you want to churn a little faster.

YIELD: ABOUT 1 GALLON

INGREDIENTS

4½ cups mashed fresh ripe peaches
2¼ cups sugar
3 eggs
¼ cup all-purpose flour
¼ teaspoon salt
3½ cups milk
2 cups half-and-half
1 cup whipping cream
1 tablespoon vanilla extract

1 Combine peaches and ¾ cup sugar; stir well and set aside.

2 Beat eggs on medium speed of an electric mixer until frothy. Combine remaining 1½ cups sugar, flour, and salt; stir well. Gradually add sugar mixture to eggs; beat until slightly thickened. Add milk; mix well.

3 Pour egg mixture into a large saucepan. Cook over low heat, stirring constantly, until mixture thickens enough to coat a metal spoon (about 15 minutes). Cover and refrigerate mixture until thoroughly chilled (about 2 hours). Stir in half-and-half, whipping cream, vanilla, and mashed peach mixture.

4 Pour into freezer container of a 1-gallon hand-turned or electric freezer. Freeze according to manufacturer's instructions. Let ripen 1–2 hours before serving.

CHILTON COUNTY PEACH MILK SHAKE

Chilton County lies in the heart of Alabama peach country. Folks in this area are known for their peach pies, peach ice cream, and especially for their outstanding peach milk shakes.

YIELD: ABOUT 4 CUPS

INGREDIENTS

1½ cups chopped fresh ripe peaches
1 tablespoon powdered sugar
1 cup milk
1½ cups vanilla or peach ice cream

Peaches are a natural source of sweetness. They may be white or yellow —choose whichever you prefer.

1 Combine peaches and powdered sugar; toss gently. Cover and refrigerate mixture for 1–6 hours. Combine peaches, milk, and ice cream in container of electric blender; process until smooth.

Always buy ripe peaches (they do not ripen after picking), and do not store for more than 2 days. Peel and pit them before use.

SHADE TREE LEMONADE

Nothing can quench thirst on a hot, humid afternoon better than a big glass of fresh lemonade. The sugar syrup base can be made ahead and kept on hand in the refrigerator.

YIELD: ABOUT 7 CUPS

INGREDIENTS

1½ cups sugar

½ cup water

grated rind of 1 lemon

1½ cups fresh lemon juice

4½ cups ice water

1 Combine sugar and ½ cup water in a small saucepan; place over low heat and stir until sugar dissolves. Remove from heat and let mixture cool. Add lemon rind, lemon juice, and ice water; mix well. Refrigerate until thoroughly chilled. Serve over ice.

MINT TEA

Hot Southern summers necessitate drinking lots of iced tea. Anyone lucky enough to have a herb garden usually grows fresh mint specifically to enjoy this refreshing libation.

YIELD: 1 QUART

INGREDIENTS

1 quart-size tea bag

¾ cup sugar (vary according to taste)

¼ cup packed fresh mint leaves

2 cups boiling water

2 cups cold water

sprigs of fresh mint

lemon slices (optional)

1 In a heatproof container, combine tea bag, sugar, and packed fresh mint leaves. Pour boiling water over tea mixture. Cover and steep 5–10 minutes. Remove and discard tea bag and mint leaves. Transfer to a tea pitcher; add cold water. Serve over ice. Garnish with sprigs of fresh mint and serve with lemon, if desired.

The menthol oils that they contain, particularly peppermint, are a natural remedy for indigestion, which is why mint tea is traditionally consumed after a rich meal.

Did you know?

For thousands of years, mint has been used for its flavor as well as its medicinal purposes. The three main types of mint commonly used are peppermint, spearmint, and apple mint.

COLD COFFEE PUNCH

In the summer, many Southerners sip their coffee cold rather than hot. This coffee punch is thick, rich, and sweet enough to serve as dessert or at your next party.

YIELD: ABOUT 16 CUPS

INGREDIENTS

2 quarts hot strong brewed coffee

⅓ cup powdered sugar

2 cups milk

2 teaspoons vanilla extract

1 pint vanilla ice cream, softened

1 pint chocolate ice cream, softened

1½ cups whipping cream, whipped

ground cinnamon

1 Combine coffee and powdered sugar, stirring until sugar dissolves. Cover and refrigerate until mixture is thoroughly chilled.

2 Combine cold coffee mixture, milk, and vanilla, stirring well. Scoop ice cream into a large punch bowl. Pour coffee mixture over ice cream, stirring gently. Top with dollops of whipped cream; sprinkle with cinnamon.

Recipes

Fall

APPALACHIAN APPLE BUTTER

Apple butter was traditionally cooked outdoors in a black kettle over a fire. This recipe simplifies the cooking process, but still captures the original flavor of the sweet spread.

YIELD: 5–6 HALF PINTS

INGREDIENTS

1 dozen medium-sized cooking apples, peeled, cored, and coarsely chopped

1½ quarts apple cider

⅓ cup red cinnamon candies (optional)

1⅓ cups sugar

1 tablespoon cider vinegar

1½ teaspoons ground cinnamon

½ teaspoon ground cloves

1 Combine apples, cider, and candies, if desired, in a Dutch oven. Bring to a boil; cover, reduce heat, and simmer for 1 hour, or until apples are tender. Drain apples; mash by hand with a potato masher, or spoon into a food processor and pulse just until smooth. Return mashed apples to Dutch oven, and add sugar, vinegar, cinnamon, and cloves. Cook, uncovered, over medium heat for 45–50 minutes, or until thickened, stirring often.

2 Remove from heat; ladle apple butter into hot sterilized jars, leaving ¼-inch of headspace. Wipe jar rims clean, and cover at once with metal lids; screw on bands. Process in a boiling-water bath for 10 minutes. See page 66 for alternative storage in a sterilized clip-lock jar.

MUSCADINE JELLY

Muscadine grapes, or scuppernongs, are unique to the southeastern United States. They have a sweet flavor and a musky odor. The jelly is a treat spread over biscuits or toast.

YIELD: 6–8 HALF PINTS

INGREDIENTS

3½ pounds muscadines (about 7 cups)

½ cup water

7 cups sugar

1 (3-ounce) package liquid pectin

1 Remove stems from grapes. Wash, sort, and place in a Dutch oven. Mash grapes by hand with a potato masher, a small amount at a time; add water. Bring mixture to a boil; cover, reduce heat, and simmer for 20 to 30 minutes. Remove from heat, and press mixture through a jelly bag, extracting 4 cups juice. Cover and let cool completely.

2 Strain juice through cheesecloth into a large Dutch oven. Add sugar; stir well. Place over high heat; cook, stirring constantly, until boiling. Add pectin; return to a full boil; boil for 1 minute, stirring constantly. Remove from heat, and skim off foam with a metal spoon.

3 Ladle hot jelly into hot sterilized jars, leaving ¼-inch of headspace; wipe jar rims, cover at once with metal lids, and screw on bands. Process in boiling-water bath for 5 minutes. See page 66 for alternative storage in a sterilized clip-lock jar.

121

CHEESE BISCUITS

Some biscuit makers wouldn't dream of using anything but self-rising flour. This particular biscuit is made even lighter with additional soda, plus buttermilk.

YIELD: 20 BISCUITS

INGREDIENTS

2–2¼ cups self-rising flour
2 teaspoons sugar
⅓ cup vegetable shortening
1 cup (4 ounces) finely shredded cheddar cheese
1 cup buttermilk
½ teaspoon baking soda
3–4 tablespoons lightly salted butter or margarine, melted

1 Combine flour and sugar; cut in shortening with a pastry blender until mixture resembles coarse meal. Stir in cheese.

2 Combine buttermilk and soda; stir well. Add buttermilk mixture to flour mixture. Stir until dry ingredients are moistened. Turn dough out onto a floured surface, and knead lightly for 1–2 minutes.

3 Roll dough out to ½-inch thickness; cut into rounds with a 2-inch biscuit cutter. Place on a lightly greased baking sheet and brush tops with a small amount of melted butter. Bake at 425° for 10–12 minutes, or until browned. Brush tops with melted butter again, if desired.

CREOLE CABBAGE

Harvested as late as November, leafy green heads of cabbage are delicious steamed and topped with butter or simmered with tomatoes, onions, and green bell pepper.

YIELD: 8 SERVINGS

INGREDIENTS

2 slices bacon, cut into 1-inch pieces

¼ cup chopped onion

¾ cup chopped green bell pepper

1 (28-ounce) can whole tomatoes, undrained and chopped

1 medium head cabbage, chopped

¼ cup cider vinegar

½ teaspoon salt

½ teaspoon black pepper

3 dashes hot sauce

1 Cook bacon in a Dutch oven over medium-high heat until crisp. Add onion and green pepper; sauté until vegetables are tender. Add tomatoes, cabbage, vinegar, salt, black pepper, and hot sauce. Cover and bring to a boil; reduce heat, and simmer for 20–25 minutes or until cabbage is tender, stirring occasionally.

GLAZED RUTABAGA

Fall brings a harvest of rutabagas bursting with distinctive flavor that is best when sweetened with a bit of sugar.

YIELD: 4–6 SERVINGS

INGREDIENTS

1 large rutabaga, peeled and cut into cubes (5–6 cups)

4 cups water

¼ cup unsalted butter or margarine

¼ cup firmly packed brown sugar

2 tablespoons lemon juice

1½ teaspoons Worcestershire sauce

¼ teaspoon salt

cracked black pepper

1 Combine rutabaga and water in a large skillet. Bring to a boil; cover, reduce heat, and simmer for 25–30 minutes, or until tender. Drain well.

2 Melt butter in skillet; stir in brown sugar, lemon juice, Worcestershire sauce, and salt. Add rutabaga; cook over medium heat, stirring constantly, for 3–4 minutes, or until rutabaga is glazed and thoroughly heated. Sprinkle with cracked black pepper before serving.

TRADITIONAL TURNIP GREENS WITH TURNIP ROOTS

You can make an entire meal out of a bowl of old-fashioned turnip greens with pot likker (the cooking liquid) and a wedge of steaming cornbread.

YIELD: 6–8 SERVINGS

INGREDIENTS

5 pounds young and tender fresh turnip greens with roots (1 large bunch)

½ pound salt pork, cut into 4 pieces

2 cups water

½ teaspoon salt

1 teaspoon sugar

hot pepper sauce (optional)

1 Wash turnip greens thoroughly; drain and wash again. Drain well. Tear greens into bite-size pieces. Peel turnip roots and coarsely chop.

2 Rinse salt pork. Combine salt pork, water, and salt in a large Dutch oven over high heat; bring to a boil. Cover, reduce heat, and simmer for 30 minutes. Stir in turnip greens; cover and cook for 20 minutes. Add turnip roots and sugar; cover and cook for 15–20 minutes or until the greens and roots reach the desired degree of doneness. Remove and discard salt pork. Serve turnips with hot sauce, if desired.

SOUTHERN SPOON BREAD

Old-fashioned spoon bread is soufflé-like on the top, but still moist on the bottom. Of course, it is served with a spoon!

YIELD: 6–8 SERVINGS

INGREDIENTS

2 cups milk

3 tablespoons unsalted butter or margarine

½ teaspoon salt

1 cup cornmeal

¾ cup water

3 eggs, separated

1 Combine milk, butter, and salt in a medium saucepan; bring to a boil over medium heat. Gradually add cornmeal, stirring constantly with a wire whisk. Remove from heat. Gradually add water, stirring well. Pour into a mixing bowl.

2 Beat egg yolks until thick and lemon-colored. Stir one-fourth of the hot mixture into the yolks; add tempered yolks back into the bowl with the remaining hot mixture, stirring constantly. Beat egg whites at high speed of an electric mixer until stiff peaks form; gently fold into cornmeal mixture using a wire whisk. Pour mixture into a greased 2-quart casserole. Bake at 375°, uncovered, for 30 minutes, or until a knife inserted in center comes out clean. Serve immediately.

COUNTRY CORNBREAD OR CORN STICKS

Cornbread is especially good served alongside fresh vegetables. This recipe makes either a skillet of cornbread, a square pan of cornbread, or a dozen or so cob-shaped corn sticks.

YIELD: 6–8 SERVINGS, OR 1½ DOZEN CORN STICKS

INGREDIENTS

1½ cups cornmeal
⅓ cup all-purpose flour
2 teaspoons baking powder
½ teaspoon baking soda
1 teaspoon sugar
½ teaspoon salt
2 eggs, beaten
1½ cups buttermilk
¼ cup vegetable oil or bacon drippings

1 Combine cornmeal, flour, baking powder, soda, sugar, and salt, stirring well. Combine eggs, buttermilk, and oil; add to cornmeal mixture, stirring just until moistened.

2 Preheat oven to 450°. Place a well-greased 8-inch cast-iron skillet, 8-inch square pan, or cast-iron corn-stick pan in oven for 4 minutes, or until hot. Remove skillet; spoon batter into skillet (filling corn-stick molds three-fourths full). Bake for 15–20 minutes, or until lightly browned.

For a great party appetizer, cut the baked cornbread into squares and serve with Appalachian Butter (*page 120)

FLORIDA HEARTS OF PALM SALAD WITH PEANUT DRESSING

Hearts of palm are harvested from the swamp cabbage palm tree. This delicacy is celebrated each year at the annual Swamp Cabbage Festival in La Belle, Florida.

YIELD: 6 SERVINGS

INGREDIENTS

⅓ cup softened vanilla ice cream

3 tablespoons mayonnaise

3 tablespoons crunchy peanut butter

2 tablespoons orange juice

1 tablespoon milk or whipping cream

2 heads Bibb lettuce, leaves separated

1 (14-ounce) can hearts of palm, drained and sliced

1 (11-ounce) can mandarin oranges, drained

½ cup drained pineapple chunks

½ cup sliced strawberries

2 tablespoons dried currants or raisins

2 teaspoon finely grated orange rind

1 Combine ice cream, mayonnaise, peanut butter, orange juice, and milk in a small bowl, stirring well. Cover and refrigerate for 1 hour.

2 Arrange lettuce leaves on six chilled salad plates. Arrange hearts of palm, orange slices, pineapple chunks, strawberries, and currants evenly over each salad. Drizzle chilled dressing mixture over each salad. Sprinkle each with orange rind.

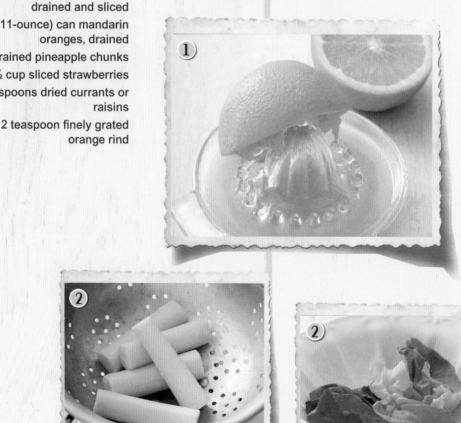

SIMPLE PEAR SALAD

This combination of tender greens, fruit, and cheese makes a first course or fruit side dish that is a refreshing addition to fall menus.

YIELD: 4 SERVINGS

INGREDIENTS

1 small head Bibb lettuce, leaves separated

4 purple kale leaves

2 very ripe fresh pears, peeled and halved or 4 canned pear halves, drained

4 tablespoons mayonnaise

4 tablespoons (1 ounce) finely shredded sharp cheddar cheese

1 Arrange lettuce and kale leaves. Top with pear halves. Place 1 tablespoon mayonnaise on top of each pear half. Sprinkle each with 1 tablespoon cheese.

Pears don't ripen well on the tree, so bought pears tend to be underripe. Place them in a cool to moderately warm room, and once ripe they should be eaten within a day as they tend to spoil quickly.

APPLE ORCHARD SALAD

Combine the full flavor of a McIntosh apple and the tartness of a Granny Smith apple in this colorful salad. Celery, raisins, and pecans contribute healthy crunch.

YIELD: 6 SERVINGS

INGREDIENTS

2 large green apples, cored, unpeeled, and diced

1 large red apple, cored, unpeeled, and diced

3 tablespoons lemon juice

½ cup chopped celery

½ cup raisins

½ cup chopped pecans, toasted

¼ cup mayonnaise

1 teaspoon sugar

lettuce leaves

1 Sprinkle apples with lemon juice and toss gently to coat; drain.

2 Combine apples, celery, raisins, and pecans, tossing gently. Combine mayonnaise and sugar, stirring well. Add mayonnaise mixture to apple mixture and stir gently. Serve over lettuce leaves.

HAM BONE & TOMATO-RICE SOUP

This is an example of a Depression era soup that fed many Southern families when times were tough. It's still a flavorful, inexpensive soup to make with a leftover ham bone.

YIELD: 6–8 SERVINGS

INGREDIENTS

1 meaty ham bone (about 1 pound)

1 (28-ounce) can stewed tomatoes, undrained

¾ cup long-grain rice, uncooked

½ teaspoon salt

French bread

1 Place ham bone in a Dutch oven. Add enough water to barely cover the bone (about 6 cups). Bring to a boil over medium heat; cover, reduce heat, and simmer for 1 hour. Remove bone from broth; cut meat from bone, and return to broth. (If desired, refrigerate broth until chilled and remove fat).

2 Bring broth mixture to a boil; add tomatoes, rice, and salt. Cover, reduce heat, and simmer for 30 minutes. Serve with French bread.

CHILI WITH BEANS

Some Southerners like their chili with chunks of beef or venison, and some add beans, while others go bean-free. This favorite version opts for ground beef and beans.

YIELD: 8–10 SERVINGS

INGREDIENTS

1 large onion, chopped
2 tablespoons vegetable oil
1½ pounds lean ground beef
2 (15-ounce) cans tomato sauce
2 (16-ounce) cans kidney beans, drained
1 (6-ounce) can tomato paste
1½ cups water
1 cup beer or water
3 tablespoons chili powder
1 teaspoon brown sugar
1 teaspoon cider vinegar
½ teaspoon salt
¼ teaspoon garlic powder
⅛ teaspoon cayenne pepper
⅛ teaspoon ground cumin
1–3 dashes hot sauce
tortilla chips

1 Sauté onion in oil in a large Dutch oven until tender. Add ground beef; cook over medium heat until browned, stirring to crumble. Drain. Add the remaining ingredients, except the tortilla chips, and simmer, uncovered, over low heat for 40–45 minutes or until desired degree of thickness. Serve with tortilla chips.

FOOTBALL BRUNSWICK STEW

This popular stew typically contains chicken and pork, potatoes, tomatoes, lima beans, and corn; it's often served on chilly evenings and at football tailgates.

YIELD: 10–12 SERVINGS

INGREDIENTS

1 (1¾-pound) pork loin roast, trimmed

4 boneless, skinless chicken breast halves (about 1⅓ pounds)

1 cup chopped onion

1 cup chopped green bell pepper

1–2 tablespoons bacon drippings or vegetable oil

4 (14½-ounce) cans tomatoes, undrained and chopped

1 (8-ounce) can tomato sauce

¼ cup sugar

3 tablespoons Worcestershire sauce

2 tablespoons cider vinegar

2 cups water

2 tablespoons all-purpose flour

1 pound red potatoes, peeled and cubed

1–2 teaspoons hot sauce

1 teaspoon salt

½ teaspoon black pepper

¼ teaspoon ground turmeric

2 (16-ounce) cans whole-kernel corn, drained

1 (16-ounce) can lima beans, drained

fresh chopped parsley

1 Combine pork roast and chicken breasts in a large kettle or Dutch oven; cover with water and bring to a boil. Cover, reduce heat, and simmer for 1½ hours, or until meats are tender. Drain and cool meats completely. Set aside.

2 Sauté onion and green pepper in bacon drippings in a large Dutch oven. Add meats, tomatoes, tomato sauce, sugar, Worcestershire sauce, and vinegar.

3 Combine water and flour, stirring well. Stir flour mixture into meat mixture. Add potatoes, hot sauce, salt, pepper, and turmeric; stir well. Cover and cook over medium heat for 30 minutes, or until potatoes are tender, stirring occasionally. Stir in corn and lima beans; cook for 15 additional minutes. Garnish with fresh chopped parsley and serve.

THANKSGIVING TURKEY & DRESSING WITH GIBLET GRAVY

Traditional turkey is usually served with cornbread dressing and sometimes this flavorful giblet gravy.

YIELD: 14–16 SERVINGS

INGREDIENTS
Turkey

1 (12–14-pound) fresh or frozen turkey

¼ cup unsalted butter or margarine, melted

1½ teaspoons salt

Cornbread Dressing (Yield: 8 servings)

2 cups cornmeal

⅓ cup all-purpose flour

1 tablespoon sugar

1 teaspoon baking powder

¼ teaspoon baking soda

¼ teaspoon salt

2 cups buttermilk

3 eggs, beaten

1 tablespoon vegetable oil

1 tablespoon vegetable oil or bacon drippings

5–6 slices white bread, crumbled

1 onion, finely chopped

2 stalks celery, finely chopped

4 cups chicken or turkey broth

1 teaspoon poultry seasoning

½ teaspoon white pepper

½ teaspoon rubbed sage

¼ teaspoon salt

¼ teaspoon black pepper

Giblet Gravy (Yield: 2½ Cups)

giblets and neck from 1 turkey

3¼ cups water

1 small onion, chopped

1 stalk celery, chopped

2 hard-cooked eggs, chopped

1 teaspoon salt

½ teaspoon black pepper

2 tablespoons cornstarch

1 Thaw turkey, if frozen. Remove giblets and neck from turkey; reserve for gravy. Rinse turkey with cold water; drain and pat dry. Tie ends of legs to tail with string, or tuck them under flap of skin around tail. Lift wing tips up and over back, and tuck under turkey.

2 Place turkey, breast side up, on a rack in a large roasting pan. Brush entire bird with melted butter; sprinkle with salt. Insert a meat thermometer in the meaty part of a thigh. Bake at 325° for 4–5 hours, or until meat thermometer registers 180°, basting with pan drippings every hour. If turkey gets too brown, tent top with aluminum foil. After roasting for 3 hours, cut string or band of skin holding legs to tail. When done, let turkey stand for 15 minutes before carving.

3 To make the cornbread dressing, combine the cornmeal, flour, sugar, baking powder, soda, and salt in a large mixing bowl. Add buttermilk, eggs, and 1 tablespoon oil, mixing well.

4 Preheat oven to 450°. Place 1 tablespoon oil or bacon drippings in a 10-inch cast-iron skillet. Place skillet in oven for 3–4 minutes. Remove pan and tilt to evenly distribute oil or drippings; pour cornbread batter into pan and bake for 25–30 minutes. Cool; crumble cornbread into a large bowl. Stir in crumbled white bread. Set aside.

5 Combine onion and celery in a small saucepan. Add 3 tablespoons chicken broth. Cook over medium heat until vegetables are just tender; add to crumbled cornbread mixture. Stir in poultry seasoning, white pepper, sage, salt, and pepper. Add enough remaining broth so that dressing mixture holds together, adjusting for desired moistness (add up to 4 cups broth for a moist dressing; less for a drier dressing). Spoon mixture into a lightly greased 13- x 9- x 2-inch baking dish. Bake at 350° for 30 to 35 minutes, or until dressing is lightly browned.

6 For the giblet gravy, cover giblets and neck with 3 cups of the water in a small saucepan. Bring to a boil; cover, reduce heat, and simmer for 1 hour, or until giblets are tender. Drain, reserving broth, and discard turkey neck. Chop giblets and return to broth in saucepan. Add onion, celery, eggs, salt, and pepper. Bring to a boil; reduce heat, and simmer, uncovered, for 30–45 minutes. Combine cornstarch and the remaining ¼ cup water, stirring well; stir into broth mixture. Bring to a boil; boil for 2 minutes.

7 Serve the carved turkey with the cornbread dressing and hot giblet gravy.

LOUISIANA JAMBALAYA

There are many versions of jambalaya, but they all seem to include three ingredients: rice, pork, and seafood. This version has just the right amount of hot, spicy flavor.

YIELD: 8–10 SERVINGS

INGREDIENTS

1 pound smoked sausage, cut into thin slices

1 cup chopped green bell pepper

½ cup chopped onion

½ cup chopped celery

2 cloves garlic, minced

1 tablespoon all-purpose flour

1 (28-ounce) can tomatoes, undrained and coarsely chopped

2½ cups water

1 cup regular long-grain rice, uncooked

1 teaspoon salt

½ teaspoon dried thyme leaves

¼ teaspoon black pepper

¼ teaspoon cayenne pepper

1 pound medium-size shrimp, peeled and deveined

1 Cook sausage in a large Dutch oven until browned. Drain off all but 2 tablespoons pan drippings. Add green pepper, onion, celery, and garlic; cook over low heat until vegetables are tender. Add flour, stirring until blended. Stir in tomatoes and water; bring to a boil. Add rice, salt, thyme, black pepper, and cayenne. Return to a boil; reduce heat and simmer, covered, for 20 minutes. Add shrimp; cover and cook for 5 minutes or until shrimp turn pink.

SHRIMP CREOLE

This creole dish from Louisiana consists of cooked shrimp simmered in a tomato sauce spiced with hot sauce and served over rice. The shrimp are cooked separately and added to the sauce at the end.

YIELD: 4 SERVINGS

INGREDIENTS

2 medium green bell peppers, chopped

1 medium onion, chopped

⅓ cup chopped celery

1 bay leaf

½ teaspoon salt

¼ teaspoon black pepper

¼ teaspoon hot sauce

3 tablespoons butter or margarine, melted

2 (16-ounce) cans diced tomatoes, undrained

1 pound medium shrimp, cooked and peeled

hot cooked long-grain rice

1 Combine bell peppers, onion, celery, bay leaf, salt, pepper, hot sauce, and butter in a Dutch oven; cook over medium heat, stirring occasionally, until vegetables are tender. Stir in tomatoes; reduce heat and simmer for 20 minutes. Add cooked shrimp; cook over low heat until thoroughly heated. Discard bay leaf. Serve immediately over rice.

COASTAL GUMBO

In New Orleans, gumbo is always on the menu. This spicy seafood stew has a roux base and is thickened with okra.

YIELD: 10–12 SERVINGS

INGREDIENTS

¾ cup vegetable oil

¾ cup all-purpose flour

2 cups chopped onion

2 cups chopped green
bell pepper

1 cup chopped celery

2 cloves garlic, minced

1 pound smoked sausage or
andouille sausage,
cut into thin slices

1 pound okra, sliced

5 cups chicken broth

3 cups water

2 cups peeled,
chopped tomatoes

1 (8-ounce) can tomato sauce

3 tablespoons Worcestershire
sauce

1 bay leaf

1–2 teaspoons hot sauce

1 teaspoon cayenne pepper

¼ teaspoon white pepper

½ teaspoon dried thyme
leaves

½ teaspoon dried oregano
leaves

1½ pounds medium-size
shrimp, peeled and deveined

1 pound fresh grouper fillets,
skinned and cut into 1-inch
pieces or ¾ pound fresh
crabmeat, drained and flaked

1 (12-ounce) container fresh
oysters, undrained

hot cooked rice

1 Combine oil and flour in a large Dutch oven; cook over medium heat, stirring constantly, until roux is dark brown (about 20 minutes). Stir in onion, green pepper, celery, and garlic; cook for 30–40 minutes, stirring frequently, until vegetables are tender. Set aside.

2 Cook sausage in a large skillet until lightly browned; drain, reserving 2 tablespoons drippings in skillet. Add sausage to vegetable mixture. Cook okra in sausage drippings over low heat until browned. Add to vegetable mixture, stirring well. Cook mixture over low heat until thoroughly heated. Add chicken broth and water, stirring well. Add tomatoes, tomato sauce, Worcestershire sauce, bay leaf, hot sauce, cayenne, white pepper, thyme, and oregano; reduce heat, and simmer 1½–2 hours, stirring occasionally.

3 Add shrimp, fish or crabmeat, and oysters to vegetable and sausage mixture. Simmer for 15–20 minutes, or until edges of oysters begin to curl and fish is done. Remove and discard bay leaf. Serve gumbo over rice.

New Orleans
FINEST SEAFOOD
1859 *138 Years Of Family Pride* 1997

OYSTER CASSEROLE

Apalachicola Bay oysters are valued for their salty-sweet flavor and meaty texture. This holiday casserole is a favorite because the oysters retain their signature flavor even after cooking.

YIELD: 6 SERVINGS

INGREDIENTS

2 (12-ounce) containers fresh oysters

¼ teaspoon salt

¼ teaspoon black pepper

⅛ teaspoon hot sauce

¼ cup chopped celery

¼ cup chopped green onion

¼ cup chopped green bell pepper

¼ cup minced fresh parsley

2 tablespoons lemon juice

2 teaspoons Worcestershire sauce

2 cups crushed soda crackers (saltine crackers)

½ cup butter, melted

½ cup half-and-half

paprika

1 Drain oysters and place half of them in a lightly greased shallow 2-quart baking dish; sprinkle with salt, pepper, and hot sauce. Top with half each of the vegetables, parsley, lemon juice, and Worcestershire sauce. Sprinkle with half the crushed crackers. Drizzle with half the butter and half-and-half.

2 Top with remaining oysters, vegetables, parsley, lemon juice, and Worcestershire sauce. Add remaining crushed crackers, butter, and half-and-half. Sprinkle paprika over all. Bake at 350° for 40 minutes, or until bubbly and lightly browned.

SMOTHERED QUAIL

Quail can be purchased at many grocery stores in the frozen foods section, but originally they were the reward of a day spent in the field with your favorite hunting dog. They taste magnificent smothered with vegetables in a white wine sauce.

YIELD: 6 SERVINGS

INGREDIENTS

12 quail, dressed
½ teaspoon salt
½ teaspoon black pepper
¾ cup all-purpose flour
vegetable oil
1½ cups chicken broth
¼ cup molasses
2 tablespoons Worcestershire sauce
1 tablespoon lemon juice
1 teaspoon poultry seasoning
½ pound fresh mushrooms, halved
4 stalks celery, cut into 1-inch pieces
4 carrots, sliced
½ cup dry white wine
¼ cup chopped green onions

1 Sprinkle quail with salt and pepper; dredge in flour. Brown quail in hot oil in a large heavy skillet. Remove quail; drain. Return quail to skillet.

2 Combine chicken broth, molasses, Worcestershire sauce, lemon juice, and poultry seasoning; stir well, and add to skillet. Bring to a boil; cover, reduce heat, and simmer for 30 minutes. Add mushrooms, celery, carrots, and wine. Cover and simmer for 30 additional minutes. Sprinkle with green onions; cook for 5 minutes.

GLAZED ORANGE ROLLS

These sweet, orange-flavored yeast rolls practically melt in your mouth. Bake them in muffin pans or square baking pans.

YIELD: 3 DOZEN

INGREDIENTS

¼ cup milk
¼ cup water
¼ cup unsalted butter or margarine
¼ cup vegetable shortening
¼ cup plus 2 tablespoons sugar
½ teaspoon salt
1 package dry yeast
½ cup warm water (105° to 115°)
1 egg
1 egg yolk
3–4 cups all-purpose flour
½ cup unsalted butter or margarine, softened
½ cup sugar
1 tablespoon grated orange rind
2 cups powdered sugar
¼ cup orange juice
1 teaspoon vanilla extract

1 Combine milk, ¼ cup water, ¼ cup butter, shortening, ¼ cup plus 2 tablespoons sugar, and salt in a saucepan; cook over low heat until butter and shortening melt. Let cool until temperature registers 105°–115° on a candy thermometer.

2 Dissolve yeast in ½ cup warm water in a large mixing bowl; let stand for 5 minutes. Stir in melted shortening mixture, egg, and egg yolk. Gradually add 2 cups flour, beating on medium speed of an electric mixer until smooth. Stir in enough remaining flour to form a soft dough.

3 Turn dough out onto a lightly floured surface, and knead until smooth and elastic (about 5–7 minutes). Place dough in a greased bowl, turning to grease top. Cover and let rise in a warm place (85°), free from drafts, for 1 hour, or until doubled in bulk. Punch dough down and divide into 2 equal portions. Roll each portion out into a 12- x 8-inch rectangle.

4 Combine ½ cup butter, ½ cup sugar, and orange rind, stirring well. Spread half of mixture over each portion of dough. Roll up each portion of dough jelly-roll fashion, beginning at long side. Pinch seams to seal. Cut each roll into 18 slices; place slices in paper-lined muffin pans or 8-inch-square baking pans. Cover and let rise in a warm place, free from drafts, for 1 hour.

5 Bake at 350° for 18–20 minutes, or until lightly browned. Combine powdered sugar, orange juice, and vanilla, stirring well. Drizzle over warm rolls.

③

④

④

MISSISSIPPI MUD SQUARES WITH COCOA FROSTING

Named for the thick mud found along the banks of the Mississippi River, these much more appealing chunky, marshmallow-studded brownies will make your mouth water.

YIELD: ABOUT 1 DOZEN

INGREDIENTS

1 cup unsalted butter
½ cup cocoa
2 cups sugar
1¼ cups all-purpose flour
1¼ cups chopped pecans
¼ teaspoon salt
4 eggs, beaten
1 teaspoon vanilla extract
2½ cups miniature marshmallows

Cocoa Frosting (Yield: 2 Cups)

½ cup unsalted butter
¼ cup plus 2 tablespoons milk
¼ cup plus 2 tablespoons cocoa
1 (16-ounce) package powdered sugar
1 teaspoon vanilla extract

1 Melt butter in a small saucepan over medium heat; add cocoa, mixing well. Remove from heat and let cool.

2 Combine sugar, flour, pecans, and salt in a large mixing bowl; stir well. Add eggs and vanilla; stir until blended. Stir in melted chocolate mixture.

3 Spoon batter into a lightly greased and floured 13- x 9- x 2-inch baking dish or pan. Bake at 350° for 30 minutes, or until a wooden pick inserted in center comes out clean. Immediately sprinkle marshmallows over top of hot brownies.

4 To make the Cocoa Frosting, combine butter, milk, and cocoa in a small saucepan; cook over medium heat, stirring frequently, until butter melts and cocoa is incorporated. Remove from heat and transfer to a medium mixing bowl. Add sugar and vanilla. Beat on low speed of an electric mixer until smooth. Spread Cocoa Frosting over marshmallows. Cool and cut into squares.

FAVORITE PEANUT BRITTLE

George Washington Carver would be pleased to taste crunchy peanut brittle. This popular candy is frequently made during the holidays.

YIELD: ABOUT 2 POUNDS

INGREDIENTS

2 cups sugar
1 cup light corn syrup
½ cup water
1 cup raw or dry-roasted peanuts
2 tablespoons unsalted butter
1 teaspoon vanilla extract
1 teaspoon baking soda
¼ teaspoon salt

1 Combine sugar, corn syrup, and ½ cup water in a large saucepan. Cook over medium-low heat, stirring constantly, until sugar dissolves. Cover and cook over medium heat for 2–3 minutes to wash down sugar crystals from sides of pan. Add peanuts; cook, uncovered, stirring frequently, until mixture reaches the hard-crack stage (300° on a candy thermometer). Stir in butter, vanilla, soda, and salt.

2 Working quickly, pour mixture into a buttered jelly roll pan; spread thinly. Let cool until firm; break into pieces. Store in airtight containers.

PUMPKIN-PECAN MUFFINS

Use fresh or canned pumpkin when making these sweet muffins. Their moist texture and spicy flavor will bring to mind the taste of spice cake or gingerbread.

YIELD: 1½ DOZEN

INGREDIENTS

¾ cup firmly packed brown sugar

2 eggs

¼ cup butter or margarine, melted

1 cup mashed, cooked fresh, or canned pumpkin

½ cup buttermilk

2 cups all-purpose flour

2 teaspoons baking powder

1 teaspoon ground cinnamon

1 teaspoon ground allspice

½ teaspoon salt

¼ teaspoon ground cloves

½ cup chopped pecans

½ cup raisins

1 Combine sugar, eggs, and butter in a large mixing bowl; stir until sugar dissolves. Add pumpkin and buttermilk; stir until smooth.

2 Combine flour, baking powder, cinnamon, allspice, salt, cloves, pecans, and raisins; add to pumpkin mixture, stirring just until all ingredients are moistened. Spoon into paper-lined muffin pans, filling two-thirds full. Bake at 400° for 20 minutes, or until golden.

PERFECT PECAN PIE

If there were a pie hall of fame, pecan pie would be featured. This pie can be topped with ice cream, a dollop of whipped cream, or served plain—all are delicious.

YIELD: PASTRY FOR ONE SINGLE-CRUST 9-INCH PIE

INGREDIENTS
Single-Crust Pie Pastry

(Note: One refrigerated piecrust can be substituted, if desired.)

1¼ cups all-purpose flour
¼ teaspoon salt
¼ cup plus 2 tablespoons vegetable shortening
4–5 tablespoons ice water

Pecan Pie Filling
(Yield: 8-10 servings)
1 cup dark corn syrup
½ cup sugar
½ cup firmly packed brown sugar
4 eggs, beaten
⅓ cup melted unsalted butter
1 teaspoon vanilla extract
pinch of salt
1 cup pecan pieces

1 Combine flour and salt in a bowl; cut in shortening with a pastry blender until mixture resembles coarse meal. Sprinkle ice water, 1 tablespoon at a time, evenly over surface, stirring with a fork, until all dry ingredients are moistened. Shape dough into a ball; cover and refrigerate until chilled. Roll dough out to ⅛-inch thickness on a lightly floured surface. Line a 9-inch pie plate with pastry; fold edges under, and flute.

2 To make the pie filling, combine corn syrup, sugar, and brown sugar, stirring well. Stir in eggs, melted butter, vanilla, and salt until well blended.

3 Sprinkle pecans in bottom of unbaked prepared pie pastry. Pour filling over pecans. Bake at 325° for 45–50 minutes, or until set, shielding edges with foil if pastry browns too quickly. Let cool before serving.

SOUR CREAM POUND CAKE

Pound cakes were originally made with a pound each of flour, butter, sugar, and eggs, but over the years, cooks have altered the ingredients. This recipe is rich with sour cream.

YIELD: ONE 10-INCH TUBE CAKE

INGREDIENTS

1 cup unsalted butter (room temperature)
½ cup vegetable shortening
3 cups sugar
5 eggs
3 cups all-purpose flour
½ teaspoon baking soda
1 (8-ounce) container sour cream
¼ cup milk
1 teaspoon vanilla extract
vanilla ice cream (optional)

1 Cream butter and shortening until light and fluffy on low speed of an electric mixer. Gradually add sugar, beating on medium speed until light and fluffy. Add eggs, one at a time, beating after each addition.

2 Combine flour and soda, stirring well with a fork. Combine sour cream and milk. Add one-third of flour mixture to butter mixture with half of the sour cream mixture. Mix on medium speed of an electric mixer until blended. Add another third of the flour mixture and mix until blended. Add remaining flour mixture, remaining sour cream mixture, and vanilla. Mix until blended.

3 Pour batter into a heavily greased and floured 10-inch tube pan. Bake at 325° for 1 hour and 10 minutes to 1 hour and 15 minutes, or until a wooden pick inserted in center comes out clean. Cool in pan for 10 minutes; turn out on a rack and cool completely. To serve, cut cake into slices and top each slice with a scoop of ice cream, if desired.

LANE CAKE WITH COCONUT-FRUIT FILLING

This treasured Southern cake looks and smells festive. The stately 3-layer cake is topped and filled with a rich mixture of pecans, coconut, raisins, cherries, and bourbon.

YIELD: ENOUGH FOR ONE 3-LAYER CAKE

INGREDIENTS
Lane Cake

1 cup unsalted butter or margarine, softened
2 cups sugar
3½ cups all-purpose flour
1 tablespoon baking powder
½ teaspoon salt
1 cup milk
1½ teaspoons vanilla extract
8 egg whites, stiffly beaten

Coconut-Fruit Filling
(Yield: enough for 3-layer cake)
12 egg yolks
1⅔ cups sugar
1 cup salted butter or margarine
1 tablespoon all-purpose flour
1½ cups finely chopped toasted pecans
1½ cups flaked coconut
1½ cups raisins
⅔ cup finely chopped maraschino cherries
⅓ cup bourbon

1 In a large bowl, cream butter until light and fluffy on low speed of an electric mixer; gradually add sugar, beating well. Combine flour, baking powder, and salt, and add to creamed mixture alternately with milk, beginning and ending with flour mixture. Mix well on medium speed after each addition. Mix in vanilla. Gently fold in egg whites.

2 Pour batter into 3 greased and floured 9-inch round cake pans. Bake at 350° for 20–25 minutes, or until a wooden pick inserted in center comes out clean. Cool in pans for 10 minutes; remove from pans and cool completely on wire racks.

3 To make the filling, combine egg yolks, sugar, butter, and flour in a 2-quart saucepan. Cook over medium heat, stirring constantly, 20 to 25 minutes, or until mixture thickens. Remove from heat and stir in pecans, coconut, raisins, cherries, and bourbon. Let cool completely, stirring occasionally, until thick enough to spread.

4 Spread filling between layers and on top of cake. If desired, filling may also be spread on sides of cake.

PECAN-TOFFEE BARS

Southern cooks excel in turning simple, ordinary ingredients into something spectacular. These dessert cookies are full of toffeelike flavor and topped with crunchy pecans.

YIELD: 6 DOZEN

INGREDIENTS

1¾ cups all-purpose flour
1 cup sugar
1 cup butter, softened
1 teaspoon vanilla extract
1 egg, separated
¾ cup finely chopped pecans

1 Lightly grease a 15- x 10- x 1-inch jellyroll pan; set aside.

2 Combine flour, sugar, butter, vanilla, and egg yolk in a large mixing bowl; beat on low speed of an electric mixer until blended, then increase to medium speed and beat until combined.

3 Pat dough evenly into prepared jellyroll pan. Lightly beat egg white; spread over top of dough evenly with a brush; sprinkle with pecans. Bake at 275° for 1 hour and 15 minutes or until golden. Immediately cut into squares; remove to wire rack to cool completely.

EASY SOUR CREAM PUMPKIN PIE

Most seasoned cooks have a favorite recipe for pumpkin pie. Usually the recipes are similar, but this one adds sour cream for a richer flavor and smoother texture.

YIELD: PASTRY FOR ONE SINGLE-CRUST 9-INCH PIE

INGREDIENTS

Single-Crust Pie Pastry
(Note: One refrigerated piecrust can be substituted, if desired.)

1¼ cups all-purpose flour
¼ teaspoon salt
¼ cup plus 2 tablespoons vegetable shortening
4–5 tablespoons ice water

Pumpkin Filling
(Yield: 6-8 servings)

¾ cup sugar
¼ cup firmly packed brown sugar
½ teaspoon ground cinnamon
½ teaspoon ground nutmeg
¼ teaspoon ground ginger
⅛ teaspoon salt
2 cups mashed cooked pumpkin
1 (8-ounce) container sour cream
3 eggs, separated

1 Combine flour and salt in a bowl; cut in shortening with a pastry blender until mixture resembles coarse meal. Sprinkle ice water, 1 tablespoon at a time, evenly over surface, stirring with a fork, until all dry ingredients are moistened. Shape dough into a ball; cover and refrigerate until chilled. Roll dough out to ⅛-inch thickness on a lightly floured surface. Line a 9-inch pie plate with pastry; fold edges under, and flute.

2 Combine sugar, brown sugar, cinnamon, nutmeg, ginger, and salt, stirring well. Add pumpkin and sour cream, stirring well.

3 Beat egg yolks until thick; stir into pumpkin mixture. Beat egg whites on medium speed of an electric mixture until stiff peaks form; fold into pumpkin mixture.

4 Pour filling into pie pastry. Bake at 400° for 10 minutes. Reduce heat to 350°, and bake for 45–50 minutes, or until set.

FESTIVE SWEET POTATO CASSEROLE

Sweet potato casserole is expected at Thanksgiving. This one is classic—creamed sweet potatoes, sugared and spiced, topped with marshmallows, and baked.

YIELD: 6–8 SERVING

INGREDIENTS
6 medium-size sweet potatoes

¼ cup sugar

¼ cup firmly packed brown sugar

2 eggs, beaten

1 teaspoon vanilla extract

½ cup unsalted butter or margarine

⅓ cup milk

1 teaspoon ground cinnamon

½ teaspoon ground nutmeg

2 cups miniature marshmallows

Research has found that sweet potatoes are one of the oldest foods in the world, existing since prehistoric times.

1 Cook sweet potatoes in boiling water for 45 minutes to 1 hour, or until tender. Cool; peel and mash by hand.

2 Combine sweet potatoes and the remaining ingredients, except marshmallows, in a bowl. Beat on medium speed of an electric mixer just until smooth. Spoon mixture into a lightly greased 11- x 7- x 2-inch baking dish or a 2-quart casserole.

Bake at 350°, uncovered, for 20 minutes. Sprinkle marshmallows over top of casserole; bake 5–10 additional minutes, or until marshmallows are lightly browned.

ELEGANT PEAR TART

Pears are not just for picking and eating. They are at their best enjoyed in this lovely, elegant pear tart.

YIELD: PASTRY FOR ONE 10-INCH TART

INGREDIENTS
Tart Pastry

(Note: One refrigerated piecrust can be substituted, if desired.)

1½ cups all-purpose flour
½ teaspoon salt
2 tablespoon sugar
¼ cup plus 2 tablespoons unsalted butter
2 tablespoons vegetable shortening
4–6 tablespoons cold milk

Pear Filling
(Yield: 6-8 servings)

4–5 medium-size ripe pears
3 tablespoons lemon juice
3 tablespoons water
2 tablespoons unsalted butter
2 tablespoons sugar
3 egg yolks
¼ cup sugar
¼ cup whipping cream
1 tablespoon all-purpose flour
1 teaspoon vanilla extract
¼ cup peach or apricot preserves

1 Combine flour, salt, and 2 tablespoons sugar in a small mixing bowl; cut in ¼ cup plus 2 tablespoons butter and shortening with a pastry blender until mixture resembles coarse meal. Sprinkle milk evenly over surface, stirring with a fork, until all ingredients are moistened. Shape dough into a ball; cover and refrigerate until chilled.

2 Roll dough out to fit a 10-inch tart pan. Prick pastry with a fork and bake at 375° for 15 minutes.

3 For the filling, peel and core pears. Combine lemon juice and water and dip pears in mixture; drain well. Cut pears in half lengthwise; cut each half into ½-inch-thick lengthwise slices. Arrange pears in prebaked tart pastry so that slices are slightly overlapping. Dot with 2 tablespoons butter and sprinkle with 2 tablespoons sugar. Set aside.

4 Combine egg yolks and ¼ cup sugar; beat well. Add cream, 1 tablespoon flour, and vanilla; beat with a wire whisk until blended, then pour over pears. Bake at 375° for 25–30 minutes or until set.

5 Cook preserves in a small saucepan over medium heat, stirring constantly, just until melted; brush over tart.

AFTER-SCHOOL OATMEAL COOKIES

Children love to be greeted after a day at school with a couple of these cookies and a glass of cold milk. The addition of corn flakes makes them super crispy.

YIELD: ABOUT 3 DOZEN

INGREDIENTS

2 cups all-purpose flour
1 teaspoon baking powder
1 teaspoon baking soda
½ teaspoon salt
½ cup unsalted butter
½ cup vegetable shortening
1 cup sugar
¼ cup firmly packed brown sugar
2 eggs
1 teaspoon vanilla extract
2 cups quick-cooking oats, uncooked
1¾ cups corn flakes

1 Combine flour, baking powder, soda, and salt; set aside.

2 Cream butter and shortening on low speed of an electric mixer until light and fluffy. Gradually add sugar and brown sugar, beating well at medium speed. Beat in eggs and vanilla. Add flour mixture, mixing well. Stir in oats and corn flakes.

3 Drop cookie dough by heaping tablespoonfuls onto lightly greased baking sheets. Bake at 325° for 12–15 minutes, or until golden. Cool slightly on baking sheets; remove to wire racks to cool completely.

CLASSIC PEANUT BUTTER COOKIES

Beginner cooks often start out learning how to make peanut butter cookies. These simple cookies are fun to make because they are rolled into balls and then flattened with a fork.

YIELD: 3 DOZEN

INGREDIENTS

¼ cup unsalted butter

¼ cup vegetable shortening

½ cup creamy peanut butter

½ cup sugar

½ cup firmly packed brown sugar

1 egg

1 teaspoon vanilla extract

1¼ cups all-purpose flour

½ teaspoon baking soda

½ teaspoon salt

1 Cream butter, shortening, and peanut butter on low speed of an electric mixer until smooth. Gradually add sugar and brown sugar, beating until light and fluffy. Add egg and vanilla, and beat well.

2 Combine flour, soda, and salt; add to creamed mixture, mixing well. Cover and refrigerate dough for 1 hour. Shape dough into 1-inch balls; place 2 inches apart on lightly greased baking sheets. Dip a fork in water and flatten cookies in a crisscross pattern to ¼-inch thickness. Bake at 350° for 10–12 minutes, or until lightly browned on edges. Let cool for 2 minutes on baking sheets, then remove to wire racks and let cool completely.

APPLE DUMPLINGS

Fall's freshest Rome or Granny Smith apples are ideal for this spectacular dessert. The apple-filled dumplings are covered with pastry and baked in sweet cinnamon syrup.

YIELD: 6 SERVINGS

INGREDIENTS

2 cups all-purpose flour
2 teaspoons sugar
¼ teaspoon salt
½ cup vegetable shortening
¼ cup unsalted butter, softened
1 egg, beaten
½ cup ice water
3 large tart cooking apples
6 teaspoons unsalted butter or margarine
3 teaspoons brown sugar
1½ teaspoons ground cinnamon
2 cups water
1½ cups sugar
3 tablespoons unsalted butter or margarine
1 teaspoon ground cinnamon
½ teaspoon ground nutmeg

1 Combine flour, 2 teaspoons sugar, and salt in a bowl; cut in shortening and ¼ cup butter with a pastry blender until mixture resembles coarse meal. Combine egg and ice water; gradually add to flour mixture, stirring with a fork to make a soft dough. Cover and refrigerate for 1 hour. On a floured surface, roll pastry out into a 21- x 14-inch rectangle; cut into six 7-inch squares.

2 Peel and core apples; cut in half, crosswise. Place one apple half (cut side down) in center of each pastry square; dot each with 1 teaspoon butter. Sprinkle each with ½ teaspoon brown sugar and ¼ teaspoon cinnamon. Moisten edges of each dumpling with a little water; bring corners to center, pinching edges to seal. Use any extra pastry to make decorative leaf designs, if desired. Place dumplings in a lightly greased 13- x 9- x 2-inch baking dish; set aside.

3 Combine 2 cups water, 1½ cups sugar, 3 tablespoons butter, 1 teaspoon cinnamon, and ½ teaspoon nutmeg in a medium saucepan; bring to a boil. Reduce heat and simmer, stirring frequently, until butter melts and sugar dissolves; set aside.

4 Bake dumplings at 450°, uncovered, for 10 minutes. Reduce heat to 350° and pour syrup mixture over dumplings. Bake for 30 additional minutes, basting occasionally.

CIDER SWEET APPLE PIE

Stayman Winesap, Red Rome, and Granny Smith are some of the South's finest cooking apples. Highlight their tart flavor by stirring apple cider into this pie.

**YIELD: PASTRY FOR ONE
DOUBLE-CRUST 9-INCH PIE**

INGREDIENTS
Double-Crust Pie Pastry
**(Note: Two refrigerated piecrusts
can be substituted, if desired.)**

3 cups all-purpose flour
1 teaspoon salt
1 cup vegetable shortening
¾ cup cold half-and-half

Cider Apple Pie Filling
(Yield: 6-8 Servings)
1 cup plus 2 tablespoons apple
cider, plus a little extra
½ cup sugar
⅓ cup firmly packed brown sugar
7½ cups peeled, cored, and sliced
cooking apples (8–9 apples)
2 tablespoons cornstarch
1 teaspoon ground cinnamon
1 tablespoon unsalted butter
or margarine
2 teaspoons milk
1 teaspoon sugar

1 Combine flour and salt in a bowl; cut in shortening with a pastry blender until mixture resembles coarse meal. Sprinkle cold half-and-half evenly over surface, stirring with a fork, until all dry ingredients are moistened. Shape dough into a ball; cover and refrigerate until chilled. Divide dough in half. Roll each half of dough to ⅛-inch thickness on a lightly floured surface. Line a 9-inch pie plate with half of the pastry; set remaining pastry aside for top of pie.

2 To make the filling, combine 1 cup apple cider, ½ cup sugar, and brown sugar in a large saucepan; bring to a boil. Add apples, and cook, uncovered, for 8 minutes, or just until apples are tender. Drain, reserving syrup. Add enough additional apple cider to syrup to measure 1⅓ cups liquid; return syrup mixture to apples in saucepan.

3 Combine cornstarch and 2 tablespoons apple cider, stirring well; add to apple mixture. Stir in cinnamon; cook, stirring constantly, until thickened. Stir in butter just until melted. Spoon mixture into prepared pie pastry. Cover with reserved top pastry. Trim edges of pastry; seal and flute edges. Cut slits in top of pastry to allow steam to escape. Brush top of pastry lightly with milk. Sprinkle top of pasty with 1 teaspoon sugar. Bake at 375° for 45–50 minutes, shielding edges with foil if pastry browns too quickly.

In recent years, scientific evidence has shown that the old proverb, "An apple a day keeps the doctor away," may be correct.

MULLED APPLE CIDER

This cider produces a spicy aroma that drifts through the house, inviting everyone into the kitchen. It's a nice addition to holiday gatherings.

YIELD: ABOUT 20 CUPS

INGREDIENTS

1 medium-size orange
2 teaspoons whole cloves
1 gallon apple cider
3 cups ginger ale
1 cup light rum or white wine
⅔ cup red cinnamon candies
3 (3-inch) cinnamon sticks

1 Cut orange into 6 wedges; stud wedges with cloves. Set aside.

2 Combine cider, ginger ale, rum, and cinnamon candies in a Dutch oven; add orange wedges and cinnamon sticks. Cook over medium heat until candies are dissolved and mixture is thoroughly heated. Serve hot.

FALL FESTIVAL PUNCH

Here is a suggestion for an easy, inexpensive punch that is just right for serving at festive fall events.

**YIELD: ABOUT
8 QUARTS**

INGREDIENTS

1½ cups honey

⅔ cup lemon juice

5 cardamom seeds

4 (3-inch) sticks cinnamon

1 teaspoon whole allspice

1 teaspoon whole cloves

1½ quarts cranberry-apple
juice

4 cups apple juice

4 cups apricot nectar

2 cups orange juice

3 quarts ginger ale

crushed ice

1 Combine honey, lemon juice, cardamom seeds, cinnamon sticks, allspice, and cloves in a small saucepan; bring to a boil, reduce heat, and simmer for 10 minutes. Strain, and discard spices. Cover and refrigerate until chilled.

2 Combine chilled mixture, cranberry-apple juice, apple juice, apricot nectar, orange juice, and ginger ale, stirring well. Serve over crushed ice.

Recipes

Winter

HOLIDAY COCKTAIL MEATBALLS

Cocktail meatballs make a fine presentation when served from a silver chafing dish. Have wooden picks handy for serving, as guests will be eager to try this sweetly sauced appetizer.

YIELD: 5 DOZEN

INGREDIENTS

1½ pounds ground beef

½ cup fine dry bread crumbs

⅓ cup minced onion

¼ cup milk

1 egg, beaten

1 tablespoon minced fresh parsley

1 tablespoon soy sauce

½ teaspoon salt

⅛ teaspoon garlic powder

⅛ teaspoon black pepper

3 tablespoons vegetable oil

2 cups currant jelly or grape jelly

1½ cups chili sauce or catsup

1 tablespoon brown sugar

2 teaspoons lemon juice

chopped green onions

1 Combine beef, bread crumbs, onion, milk, egg, parsley, soy sauce, salt, garlic powder, and pepper in a large mixing bowl; shape into 1-inch meatballs. Cook in oil over medium heat for 10–15 minutes, or until browned. Drain on paper towels.

2 Combine jelly, chili sauce, brown sugar, and lemon juice in a medium saucepan; stir well. Add meatballs; simmer for 10 minutes. Garnish with chopped green onions, and serve in a chafing dish with wooden toothpicks.

PARTY CHEESE CANNONBALL

Cheese balls appear quite often at holiday parties. Although ingredients vary slightly from hostess to hostess, this tried-and-true appetizer is always a hit.

YIELD: ONE 5-INCH CHEESE BALL (3 CUPS)

INGREDIENTS

2 (8-ounce) packages cream cheese, softened

2 cups (8 ounces) shredded sharp cheddar cheese

3 tablespoons finely chopped pimiento-stuffed olives

2 tablespoons finely chopped pimiento, drained

1 tablespoon grated onion

1 tablespoon finely minced green bell pepper

1 tablespoon Worcestershire sauce

2 teaspoons lemon juice

½ teaspoon hot sauce

¼ teaspoon cayenne pepper

¼ teaspoon salt

1½ cups finely chopped pecans, toasted

1 Combine cream cheese and cheddar cheese in a large mixing bowl; beat on medium speed of an electric mixer until blended. Stir in olives, pimiento, onion, green pepper, Worcestershire sauce, lemon juice, hot sauce, cayenne, and salt. Shape mixture into a ball; roll ball in chopped pecans to lightly coat. Wrap in plastic wrap and refrigerate overnight. Serve at room temperature.

BACON ROLL-UPS

The characteristic salty taste of bacon makes this a flavorful and economical cocktail snack.

YIELD: 50 APPETIZERS

INGREDIENTS

2 (3-ounce) packages cream cheese, softened

2 tablespoons grated onion

1 tablespoon milk

1 teaspoon mayonnaise

25 slices whole-wheat sandwich bread, cut in half, crusts removed

25 slices bacon, cut in half

1 Combine cream cheese, onion, milk, and mayonnaise, stirring until smooth. Spread cream cheese mixture evenly on each slice of bread. Starting at the short end, roll each slice up tightly. Wrap each roll-up with half a slice of bacon, securing with a wooden pick.

2 Place roll-ups on a broiler pan; bake at 350° for 30 minutes, turning, if needed, to brown bacon. Drain on paper towels.

STUFFED SWEET POTATOES

Vardaman, Mississippi, calls itself "The Sweet Potato Capital of the World," but this vitamin-packed vegetable has always been celebrated at dining tables across the entire South.

YIELD: 6 SERVINGS

INGREDIENTS

6 medium-size sweet potatoes
½ cup orange juice
3 tablespoons butter or margarine, softened
2 tablespoons honey
pinch of salt
pinch of ground nutmeg
ground cinnamon
½ cup chopped pecans

1 Wash and scrub sweet potatoes with a stiff brush; place on rack in oven and bake at 375° for 1 hour or until tender when tested with a fork. Allow potatoes to cool; cut a 1-inch lengthwise strip from top of each potato. Carefully scoop out pulp, leaving shells intact.

2 Combine potato pulp, orange juice, and butter in a large mixing bowl; beat on medium speed of an electric mixer until fluffy. Stir in honey, salt, and nutmeg. Stuff shells with potato mixture; sprinkle with cinnamon and pecans. Bake at 375° for 10–12 minutes, or until pecans are toasted.

TURNIP & CARROT TOSS

Turnips, which are really the roots of turnip greens, have white skin with a purple collar. They combine beautifully with carrots in this festive vegetable side dish.

YIELD: 6 SERVINGS

INGREDIENTS

3 medium turnips, peeled and diced (3 cups)

3 cups peeled and diced carrots

¼ cup butter or margarine, melted

2 tablespoons minced fresh parsley

2 teaspoons sugar

½ teaspoon salt

dash of black pepper

1 Place turnips and carrots in a medium saucepan and cover with a small amount of water. Bring to a boil; cover, reduce heat, and simmer for 20 minutes, or until vegetables are tender. Drain well. Add butter, parsley, sugar, salt, and pepper; toss well.

COLLARDS WITH BACON

Collard greens are a familiar vegetable in Southern cuisine. They are typically seasoned with ham hocks, fatback, or bacon, and often eaten along with black-eyed peas and cornbread.

YIELD: 8 SERVINGS

INGREDIENTS

8 slices bacon

2 cups chopped onion

2 teaspoons minced garlic

4 (1-pound) packages fresh collard greens, cleaned, trimmed, and chopped

1 (14-ounce) can chicken broth

1 teaspoon salt

½ teaspoon black pepper

¼ teaspoon dried crushed red pepper

1 Cook bacon in a Dutch oven over medium-high heat for 8–10 minutes or until crisp; remove bacon, and drain on paper towels, reserving drippings in pan. Crumble bacon; set aside.

2 Sauté onion in hot bacon drippings until tender. Add garlic and cook, stirring constantly for 30 seconds. Add collards, chicken broth, and remaining ingredients. Bring mixture to a boil; cover, reduce heat, and simmer for 1 hour, or until collards are tender. Stir crumbled bacon into collards just before serving.

PECAN-GLAZED BRUSSELS SPROUTS

Two tips for better brussels sprouts: Small sprouts are more tender and less bitter than large ones, and a shallow "X" cut into the base of each sprout helps them cook more evenly.

YIELD: 6 SERVINGS

INGREDIENTS

1½ pounds fresh brussels sprouts

½ cup water

¼ cup unsalted butter or margarine

⅓ cup firmly packed brown sugar

3 tablespoons soy sauce

¼ teaspoon salt

½ cup finely chopped pecans, toasted

1 Wash brussels sprouts thoroughly, and remove discolored leaves. Cut off stem ends, and slash bottom of each sprout with a shallow "X." Bring ½ cup water to a boil in a large saucepan; add brussels sprouts. Cover, reduce heat, and simmer for 8 to 10 minutes, or until sprouts are crisp-tender; drain and set aside.

2 Melt butter in a medium skillet; stir in brown sugar, soy sauce, and salt. Bring butter mixture to a boil, stirring constantly. Add pecans; reduce heat, and simmer, uncovered, for 5 minutes, stirring occasionally. Add brussels sprouts; cook over medium heat for 5 minutes; stir well before serving.

SEASONED NAVY BEANS

Frugal Southern cooks knew that a package of dried beans on the pantry shelf meant a savory, filling main dish could be assembled without much expense.

YIELD: 6 SERVINGS

INGREDIENTS

1 (16-ounce) package dried navy beans, soaked and drained

1½ cups cubed lean salt pork or ham

1½ cups chopped onion

2 cloves garlic, minced

1 teaspoon salt

½ teaspoon dried red pepper flakes

½ cup chopped fresh parsley

1 Place beans in a Dutch oven; add enough water to cover 2 inches above beans; cover and bring to a boil. Reduce heat, and simmer for 30 minutes. Drain and rinse beans well. Set aside.

2 Place pork in Dutch oven; cook over low heat until evenly browned. Remove pork and set aside, reserving drippings in pan. Sauté onion and garlic in drippings until tender. Add beans, pork, salt, and red pepper; cover with water and cook over low heat for 1½–2 hours, or until beans are tender, stirring occasionally. Stir in parsley.

CITRUS-AVOCADO SALAD WITH HONEY DRESSING

Florida is one of the largest producers of oranges, grapefruits, and avocados in the country. Enjoy all three fruits at once in this pretty salad.

YIELD: 6–8 SERVINGS

INGREDIENTS

4 cups torn spinach leaves
4 cups torn romaine lettuce
1 cup torn iceberg lettuce
2 oranges, peeled and sectioned, membranes removed
1 grapefruit, peeled and sectioned, membranes removed
1 avocado, peeled and sliced
1 tablespoon lemon juice
1 small onion, sliced and separated into rings
½ cup sliced celery
½ cup coarsely chopped pecans, toasted

Honey Dressing

⅓ cup sugar
2½ tablespoons lemon juice
2½ tablespoons honey
2 tablespoons cider vinegar
½ teaspoon dry mustard
½ teaspoon paprika
¼ teaspoon salt
⅛ teaspoon celery seeds
½ cup vegetable oil

1 Combine spinach, romaine, and iceberg lettuce in a large bowl; toss gently. Arrange orange sections and grapefruit sections over salad greens. Toss avocado slices gently with lemon juice; discard lemon juice. Arrange avocado, onion, and celery over salad. Sprinkle with pecans.

2 To make the dressing, combine all ingredients, except oil, in container of an electric blender; process until smooth. While blender is running, slowly pour in oil; continue to process for a few seconds until blended. Serve Honey Dressing over salad.

GRITS & SAUSAGE CASSEROLE

Fresh, stone-ground grits, made by grinding mature corn kernels, are still available in some areas of the South. This recipe uses quick-cooking grits, which can be purchased in most grocery stores.

YIELD: 8 SERVINGS

INGREDIENTS

1 cup uncooked quick-cooking grits

1 pound mild bulk pork sausage

8 eggs, beaten

1½ cups milk

¼ teaspoon garlic salt

¼ teaspoon white pepper

3 tablespoons lightly salted butter or margarine

2 cups (8 ounces) shredded sharp cheddar cheese

1 Cook grits according to package directions. Set aside.

2 Cook sausage over medium heat until browned, stirring to crumble. Drain well and set aside.

3 Combine eggs, milk, garlic salt, and white pepper in a large bowl. Stir in cooked grits. Add butter and cheese, stirring until cheese melts. Stir in sausage. Spoon mixture into a lightly greased 3-quart casserole. Bake at 350°, uncovered, for 1 hour, or until set.

UPTOWN GRITS

This recipe dresses up regular grits with a mixture of bacon, green pepper, onion, celery, and tomatoes. The combination is addictive, so be prepared to offer second helpings.

YIELD: 6–8 SERVINGS

INGREDIENTS

6 slices bacon
1 clove garlic, minced
1 cup chopped green bell pepper
½ cup chopped onion
½ cup chopped celery
1 (16-ounce) can stewed tomatoes, undrained
2 dashes hot sauce
6 cups water
1 teaspoon salt
1½ cups uncooked regular grits

1 Cook bacon in a large skillet until crisp; remove bacon, reserving 2 tablespoons drippings in skillet. Drain and crumble bacon; set aside.

2 Sauté garlic, green pepper, onion, and celery in drippings over medium heat until tender; stir in tomatoes and hot sauce. Bring mixture to a boil; reduce heat to low, and simmer for 30 minutes, stirring occasionally. Set aside.

3 Combine water and salt in a large saucepan; bring to a boil. Stir in grits with a wire whisk. Cook over low heat, stirring occasionally, for 10–20 minutes, or until grits become thick. Remove from heat; stir in tomato mixture and crumbled bacon. Serve immediately.

RED BEANS & RICE

This signature Creole dish was originally made on Mondays with beans and pork bones left from Sunday dinner. To control the spicy hot flavor, vary the amount of hot sauce.

YIELD: 6 SERVINGS

INGREDIENTS

1 pound dried red kidney beans

1–1½ pounds smoked meaty ham hocks

2 cups chopped onion

2 cups chopped celery

2 cups chopped green bell pepper

¼ cup chopped fresh parsley

1 (8-ounce) can tomato sauce

3 bay leaves

1 teaspoon white pepper

1 teaspoon dried thyme leaves

1 teaspoon garlic powder

1 teaspoon dried oregano leaves

1 teaspoon cayenne pepper

½ teaspoon salt

½ teaspoon black pepper

½–1 teaspoon hot sauce

1 pound andouille or other smoked sausage, cut into ½ inch pieces

hot cooked rice

1 Sort and wash beans; place in a soup kettle or large Dutch oven. Add water until beans are covered by 2 inches; let soak overnight. Drain and rinse beans. Add enough water to barely cover beans. Add remaining ingredients, except sausage and rice; bring to a boil over high heat. Cover tightly, reduce heat, and simmer for 1 hour and 45 minutes.

2 Remove ham hocks, and set aside. Add sausage to mixture. Cook, uncovered, over low heat for 40 minutes, stirring occasionally. Remove and discard bay leaves. Return meaty portion of ham hocks to bean mixture; stir well. Cook, uncovered, until thoroughly heated and mixture is desired thickness. Serve bean mixture over rice.

SATURDAY NIGHT BEEF STEW

Stews are usually cooked in less liquid than soups, and are typically thickened with flour. This chunky beef and vegetable combo may require a fork as well as a spoon.

YIELD: 8 SERVINGS

INGREDIENTS

¼ cup plus 3 tablespoons all-purpose flour

2 teaspoons salt

1 teaspoon black pepper

2 pounds boneless beef chuck, cut into 1-inch cubes

3 tablespoons vegetable oil

1 small onion, sliced

1 teaspoon Worcestershire sauce

2 cloves garlic, minced

2 small bay leaves

5 cups water

4 medium potatoes, peeled and quartered

4 large carrots, scraped and cut into 2-inch pieces

4 small onions, cut into quarters

2 medium turnips, peeled and quartered

3 stalks celery, cut into 2-inch pieces

¼ cup water

1 Combine ¼ cup of the flour, salt, and pepper in a bowl. Dredge meat in flour mixture and shake off excess. Heat oil in a large soup kettle or Dutch oven and brown meat on all sides. Add sliced onion, Worcestershire sauce, garlic, bay leaves, and 5 cups water; stir, and bring mixture to a boil over high heat. Cover, reduce heat to low, and simmer for 2 hours. Remove and discard bay leaves.

2 Add potatoes, carrots, quartered onions, turnips, and celery; cover and cook over low heat for 15–20 minutes, or until vegetables are tender.

3 Combine ¼ cup water and the remaining 3 tablespoons flour, stirring until smooth. Stir flour mixture into stew; cook until mixture is slightly thickened.

VEGETABLE, BEAN & SAUSAGE SOUP

When cold winter nights arrive with a hint of frost in the air, it's time to make soup. This easy-to-make recipe is filling; add crusty Icebox Rolls and a salad for a complete meal.

YIELD: 8–10 SERVINGS

INGREDIENTS

1 pound bulk pork sausage

1 large onion, chopped

½ cup chopped green bell pepper

½ cup chopped celery

2 (16-ounce) cans kidney beans, drained

1 (28-ounce) can tomatoes, undrained and chopped

4 cups water

1 (8-ounce) can tomato sauce

½ teaspoon salt

¼ teaspoon garlic powder

¼ teaspoon dried thyme leaves

¼ teaspoon black pepper

1 cup peeled and diced red potato

1 large carrot, scraped and thinly sliced

Icebox Rolls (*page 190)

1 Brown sausage in a large Dutch oven over high heat, stirring to crumble. Drain, reserving 1 tablespoon pan drippings; set sausage aside. Add onion, green pepper, and celery to drippings; sauté until tender. Add kidney beans, tomatoes, water, tomato sauce, salt, garlic powder, thyme, and black pepper, stirring well. Bring to a boil over high heat; cover, reduce heat, and simmer for 30 minutes. Add potato, carrot, and cooked sausage; cover and simmer for 30 minutes, or until vegetables are tender.

2 Serve the soup immediately with hot ice box rolls.

ICEBOX ROLLS

Shaped in the classic Parker House-style, these yeast rolls are wonderful served hot from the oven.

YIELD: 3 DOZEN

INGREDIENTS

1 cup water
⅓ cup unsalted butter or margarine
½ cup solid vegetable shortening
¾ cup sugar
1½ teaspoons salt
2 packages active dry yeast
1 cup warm water (105°–115°)
2 eggs, beaten
6 cups all-purpose flour

1 Combine 1 cup water, butter, shortening, sugar, and salt in a small saucepan; place over low heat until butter and shortening melt. Let cool until temperature registers 105°–115° on a candy thermometer.

2 Dissolve yeast in 1 cup warm water in a large mixing bowl; let stand for 5 minutes. Stir in cooled melted shortening mixture and eggs. Gradually add 2 cups flour, beating on medium speed of an electric mixer until smooth. Stir in enough remaining flour to form a thick dough. Turn dough out onto a floured surface, and knead for 5–8 minutes, or until smooth and elastic. Place in a well-greased bowl, turning to grease top; cover and refrigerate for 1½-2 hours.

3 Punch dough down; turn dough out onto a lightly floured surface. Roll to ¼ –inch thickness. Cut rounds with 2½-inch cutter. With the dull edge of a knife, make a crease just off center on each round. Fold over so that top overlaps slightly; gently press edges together.

4 Place on lightly greased baking sheets. Cover and let rise in a warm place (85°), free from drafts, for 1 hour, or until doubled in bulk.

5 Bake at 400° for 12–15 minutes, or until golden.

HOPPIN' JOHN

According to Southern lore, if black-eyed peas are eaten on New Year's Day, good luck will follow. Hoppin' John, accompanied by a skillet of cornbread, is the traditional way these good-luck peas are enjoyed.

YIELD: 8 SERVINGS

INGREDIENTS

2 cups dried black-eyed peas

¼ pound salt pork, cut into small cubes

⅔ cup chopped onion

½ cup chopped green bell pepper

⅓ cup chopped carrot

⅓ cup chopped celery

2½ cups water

1 cup regular long-grain rice, uncooked

1 bay leaf

½ teaspoon salt

¼ teaspoon dried hot red pepper flakes

¼ teaspoon dried thyme leaves

2 tablespoons chopped green onions

1 Sort and wash black-eyed peas; place in a Dutch oven. Add water until peas are covered by 2 inches. Let soak overnight.

2 Drain and rinse peas and return to the Dutch oven; add enough water to barely cover peas. Add salt pork, onion, green pepper, carrot, and celery to peas. Cover and bring to a boil over high heat. Reduce heat to low; simmer for 1½–2 hours, or until peas are tender and water has mostly cooked out.

3 Add 2½ cups additional water, rice, bay leaf, salt, red pepper flakes, and thyme to peas. Cover and cook over low heat for 20–30 minutes, or until rice is done, adding additional water if necessary. Sprinkle with green onions before serving.

HAM WITH RED-EYE GRAVY

Though it is no longer made with regularity, fried ham topped with red-eye gravy was standard breakfast fare in early Southern homes. Coffee gives the gravy a rich copper-red color.

YIELD: 4–8 SERVINGS

INGREDIENTS

4 (¼-inch) slices ham (about 1½ pounds)

1 cup water

¼ cup coffee

1 Place ham slices in an ungreased cast-iron skillet; cook slices over low heat until browned, turning occasionally. Remove ham, reserving pan drippings; drain ham on paper towels, then place on serving platter.

2 Add water and coffee to drippings in skillet. Bring coffee mixture to a boil, stirring constantly. Remove from heat; spoon gravy over ham.

APPLE-BAKED PORK ROAST

The main source of meat for early Southern farmers was the hog, and one of the prized cuts was the pork loin. This loin roast is easy to prepare and perfect for company.

YIELD: 8–10 SERVINGS

INGREDIENTS

1 (4–5-pound) rolled boneless
pork loin roast
1 teaspoon dried whole
rosemary, crushed
½ teaspoon salt
½ teaspoon garlic powder
3 tablespoons apple jelly
2 tablespoons honey mustard
2 tablespoons apple juice
1 tablespoon brown sugar
cooked broccoli
whole roast garlic

1 Place roast, fat side up, on a rack in a shallow roasting pan. Rub roast with rosemary; sprinkle with salt and garlic powder. Insert meat thermometer, making sure it does not touch fat. Bake at 325° for 1 hour and 45 minutes.

2 Combine apply jelly, honey mustard, apple juice, and brown sugar, stirring well. Brush roast with jelly mixture. Continue to bake at 325° for 15–30 minutes, or until thermometer registers 160°. Serve with broccoli and whole roast garlic.

BUTTERMILK PRALINES

The French brought pralines to Louisiana, where chefs added pecans and milk to the confection. Proper pralines should have a creamy consistency, similar to fudge.

YIELD: ABOUT 2 DOZEN

INGREDIENTS

1¾ cups sugar

¼ cup firmly packed brown sugar

1 teaspoon baking soda

1 cup buttermilk

1 teaspoon vanilla extract

1 tablespoon lightly salted butter

2 cups pecan halves

1 Butter a sheet of wax paper and set aside. Butter the sides of a Dutch oven.

2 Combine sugar, brown sugar, baking soda, and buttermilk in the Dutch oven. Slowly bring mixture to a boil over low heat, stirring constantly, until sugar dissolves. Cover, increase heat to medium, and cook for 2–3 minutes to wash down sugar crystals from sides of pan. Uncover and continue cooking, stirring occasionally, until mixture reaches soft-ball stage (234°) on a candy thermometer. Remove from heat; add vanilla, butter, and pecans. Beat vigorously with a wooden spoon until mixture just becomes glossy and begins to thicken. Working rapidly, drop mixture by heaping tablespoonfuls onto buttered wax paper; let stand until cool. Remove and store in an airtight container.

BOURBON BALLS

Make these simple, no-cook confections ahead and store until ready to serve. Their bourbon aroma adds a festive spirit to holiday gatherings.

YIELD: ABOUT 3 DOZEN

INGREDIENTS

1¼ cups finely crushed vanilla wafer crumbs

1¼ cups sifted powdered sugar

1 cup finely chopped pecans

2 tablespoons cocoa

2 tablespoons light corn syrup

3–4 tablespoons bourbon

sugar

1 Combine vanilla wafer crumbs, powdered sugar, pecans, and cocoa; mix well. Combine corn syrup and bourbon; mix well and stir into crumb mixture. Cover and refrigerate mixture for at least 30 minutes. Shape into 1-inch balls; roll each in sugar. Store in an airtight container.

GINGERBREAD MEN

Children love to decorate these fun cookies. Add a face and clothing using candies and frosting—
the possibilities are endless!

YIELD: 2–3 DOZEN

INGREDIENTS

½ cup solid vegetable shortening
½ cup firmly packed brown sugar
½ cup molasses
1 egg
3½ cups all-purpose flour
1 teaspoon baking powder
½ teaspoon baking soda
¼ teaspoon salt
1 teaspoon ground ginger
½ teaspoon ground cinnamon
½ teaspoon ground cloves
½ cup buttermilk

your choice of decoration. i.e.
chocolate-covered candies,
cinnamon candies, frosting, or
golden raisins

1 Cream shortening on low speed of an electric mixer. Gradually add sugar, beating at medium speed until light and fluffy. Beat in molasses and egg. Combine flour, baking powder, soda, salt, and spices, stirring well. Add to creamed mixture alternately with buttermilk, beginning and ending with flour mixture, stirring well after each addition. Shape dough into a ball; cover and refrigerate for at least 2 hours.

2 Roll dough out onto a lightly floured surface to ¼-inch thickness; cut with a 3–4-inch gingerbread-man cutter. Place on lightly greased baking sheets. Bake at 375˚ for 10 minutes. Let cool slightly on wire wracks, then decorate as you wish, using chocolate-covered candies, cinnamon candies, frosting, or golden raisins to create the eyes and mouth and buttons or clothing.

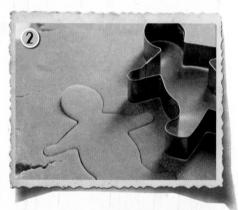

ORANGE SHORTCAKES

Here is Florida's wintertime equivalent to strawberry shortcake. The flaky shortcakes are very similar to lightly sweetened biscuits.

YIELD: 4 SERVINGS

INGREDIENTS

1 cup all-purpose flour
1 tablespoon sugar
1 teaspoon baking powder
¼ teaspoon salt
¼ cup plus 2 tablespoons unsalted butter
3–4 tablespoons milk
whipped cream

Orange Sauce
(Yield: 3-4 Cups)

7 large navel oranges
⅓ cup sugar
2 tablespoons unsalted butter or margarine
1½ teaspoons cornstarch
⅓ cup water
½ teaspoon lemon juice
½ teaspoon grated orange rind

1 Combine flour, 1 tablespoon sugar, baking powder, and salt in a bowl; cut in butter with a pastry blender until mixture resembles coarse meal. Gradually add enough milk to the mixture to form a soft dough, stirring just until dry ingredients are moistened. Turn dough out onto a lightly floured surface and knead lightly 4 or 5 times.

2 Roll dough out to ⅝ -inch thickness; cut into four 3-inch circles. Place circles on lightly greased baking sheets. Bake at 450° for 8–10 minutes, or until lightly browned. Let cool completely on wire racks.

3 To make the sauce, peel and section oranges over a bowl to catch juice; reserve ⅓ cup juice.

4 Combine reserved juice and remaining ingredients in a medium saucepan. Cook over low heat, stirring constantly, until slightly thickened and bubbly. Remove from heat; stir in orange sections.

5 Split cooled shortcakes horizontally with a fork and gently pull apart. Place bottom half of each shortcake, cut side up, on each of four dessert plates; top with Orange Sauce. Cover with top half of each shortcake, cut side down. Spoon remaining sauce over each shortcake. Decorate each with a dollop of whipped cream.

THUMBPRINT COOKIES

These cookies are filled with strawberry preserves, but they would be equally tempting filled with your favorite jam or jelly.

YIELD: 3½ DOZEN

INGREDIENTS

1 cup unsalted butter or
margarine, softened
¾ cup sugar
2 egg yolks
1 teaspoon vanilla extract
2⅓ cups all-purpose flour
¼ teaspoon salt
powdered sugar
strawberry preserves

1 Cream butter on low speed of an electric mixer; gradually add sugar, beating on medium speed until light and fluffy. Add egg yolks, beating well. Stir in vanilla.

2 Combine flour and salt, stirring well; add to creamed mixture, mixing well. Cover and refrigerate dough for 2 hours.

3 Roll dough into 1-inch balls; place balls about 2 inches apart on ungreased baking sheets. Press thumb in each ball of dough, leaving an indentation. Bake at 300° for 20–25 minutes, or until lightly browned around edges. Cool cookies on wire racks. Sprinkle cookies with powdered sugar. Place ¼ teaspoon strawberry preserves in each cookie indentation.

GINGERBREAD CAKE WITH LEMON SAUCE

Sometimes gingerbread is referred to as a "hot water" cake, since hot water is added for moisture. Dress up this simple dessert by spooning lemon sauce over each serving.

YIELD: 9 SERVINGS

INGREDIENTS

½ cup unsalted butter or margarine

¼ cup sugar

¼ cup firmly packed brown sugar

1 egg, beaten

⅔ cup light molasses

2¼ cups all-purpose flour

1½ teaspoons baking soda

½ teaspoon salt

2 teaspoons ground ginger

½ teaspoon ground nutmeg

½ teaspoon ground cinnamon

¼ teaspoon ground cloves

1 cup hot water

Lemon Sauce
(Yield: 9 Servings)

½ cup sugar

1 tablespoon cornstarch

1 cup boiling water

2 tablespoons unsalted butter or margarine

2 tablespoons lemon juice

1 teaspoon grated lemon rind

1 Cream butter on low speed of an electric mixer. Gradually add sugar and brown sugar, beating on medium speed until light and fluffy. Add egg and molasses, mixing well. Combine flour, soda, salt, and spices; add to creamed mixture alternately with hot water, beginning and ending with flour mixture. Mix well.

2 Pour batter into a lightly greased and floured 9-inch-square baking pan. Bake at 350° for 35 minutes, or until a wooden pick inserted in center comes out clean. Let cool completely in pan on a wire rack. Cut into squares or wedges.

3 For the sauce, combine sugar and cornstarch in a small saucepan. Gradually stir in boiling water. Cook over low heat, stirring constantly, until smooth and thickened. Remove from heat; add butter, lemon juice, and lemon rind, stirring until butter melts. Serve over gingerbread squares.

CHESS PIE

Perhaps this pie was named after a piece of furniture early cooks called a pie chest. Or maybe it got its name because it was rather plain and described as "just pie," which later morphed into "chess."

YIELD: 6–8 SERVINGS

INGREDIENTS

1½ cups sugar
1 tablespoon cornmeal
¼ teaspoon salt
4 eggs, beaten
1½ teaspoons vanilla extract
¼ cup milk
¼ cup unsalted butter or margarine, melted
Single-Crust Pie Pastry (*page 152), unbaked

1 Combine sugar, cornmeal, and salt in a small bowl; mix well. Combine eggs and vanilla in a medium bowl; beat well. Add sugar mixture, milk, and butter to egg mixture; beat until smooth.

2 Line a 9-inch pie plate with pastry; trim and flute edges. Pour in filling. Bake at 350° for 30 minutes, or until set.

PLEASANT HILL LEMON BREAD

In the 1800s', there was a large settlement of Shakers in Pleasant Hill, Kentucky. Their food was simple, but very good; they excelled in homemade breads like this one shared from their recipe files.

YIELD: 1 LOAF

INGREDIENTS

½ cup solid vegetable shortening
1 cup sugar
2 eggs
1½ cups all-purpose flour
1½ teaspoons baking powder
¼ teaspoon salt
½ cup milk
grated rind of 1 lemon
⅓ cup sugar
2 tablespoons lemon juice

1 Combine shortening and 1 cup sugar, creaming until light and fluffy. Add eggs, one at a time, beating well after each addition. Combine flour, baking powder, and salt; add to creamed mixture alternately with milk, mixing well after each addition. Stir in lemon rind.

2 Pour batter into a greased and floured 9- x 5- x 3-inch loaf pan. Bake at 350° for 60 minutes or until a wooden pick inserted in center comes out clean.

3 Combine ⅓ cup sugar and 2 tablespoons lemon juice, stirring until sugar dissolves; pour over bread. Cool bread in pan 10–15 minutes before removing.

LEGACY FRUITCAKE

This holiday fruitcake keeps for quite a long time if wrapped in brandy-soaked cheesecloth and placed in a tightly covered container. Add more brandy every seven days to keep it moistened.

YIELD: ONE 10-CAKE

INGREDIENTS

1½ cups lightly salted butter, softened

¾ cup sugar

¾ cup firmly packed brown sugar

½ cup molasses

7 eggs, beaten

3½ cups all-purpose flour

3½ cups yellow, green, and red candied pineapple, chopped

2¾ cups red and green candied cherries, quartered

2 cups pecans, coarsely chopped and toasted

2 cups walnuts, coarsely chopped

1½ cups raisins

1 teaspoon ground cinnamon

½ teaspoon ground allspice

½ teaspoon ground cloves

¼ cup brandy

additional brandy

1 Draw a circle with a 10-inch diameter on a piece of parchment paper or brown paper (not recycled), using a large, deep tube pan as a guide. Cut out circle; set tube pan insert in center, and draw around inside tube. Cut out smaller circle. Grease one side of paper, and set aside. Heavily grease and flour a deep 10-inch tube pan; set aside.

2 In a large bowl, cream butter until fluffy on low speed of an electric mixer. Gradually add sugar and brown sugar, beating well on medium speed. Add molasses, beating well. Alternately add beaten eggs and 3 cups of the flour to creamed mixture, beating well after each addition.

3 Combine candied pineapple, cherries, pecans, walnuts, and raisins in a large bowl; sprinkle with the remaining ½ cup flour, cinnamon, allspice, and cloves, stirring to coat well. Stir mixture into batter.

4 Spoon batter into prepared pan, pressing firmly, if necessary. Cover pan with the 10-inch paper circle, greased side down. Bake at 250° for 4 hours, or until a wooden pick inserted comes out clean. Remove from oven. Discard paper circle. Carefully loosen cake from pan and invert onto a wire rack. Pour ¼ cup brandy evenly over cake. Cool cake completely. Wrap cake in brandy-soaked cheesecloth, and store in an airtight container for up to 3 weeks. Continue to pour a small amount of brandy over cake every 7 days.

TEXAS SHEET CAKE

Some Texans attribute this cake to Lady Bird Johnson. The cake is light in texture, big on sweetness, and makes a popular addition to family gatherings.

YIELD: 12–15 SERVINGS

INGREDIENTS

2 cups all-purpose flour
2 cups sugar
¼ cup cocoa
1 teaspoon baking soda
1 cup water
½ cup butter or margarine
½ cup solid vegetable shortening
½ cup buttermilk
2 eggs
1 teaspoon vanilla extract

Chocolate-Pecan Frosting (Yield: 4 Cups)
½ cup butter or margarine
¼ cup cocoa
⅓ cup milk
1 (16-ounce) package powdered sugar
1 teaspoon vanilla extract
1 cup chopped pecans, lightly toasted

1 Combine flour, sugar, cocoa, and soda in a large mixing bowl, stirring well to combine; set aside. Combine water, butter, and shortening in a heavy saucepan; cook over medium heat, stirring constantly with a wire whisk until butter melts. Whisk in buttermilk, eggs, and vanilla until combined. Pour chocolate mixture over flour mixture, stirring well.

2 Pour batter into a lightly greased and floured 13- x 9- x 2-inch baking pan. Bake at 400° for 25 to 30 minutes, or until a wooden pick inserted in center comes out clean. Cool cake.

3 Combine butter, cocoa, and milk in a medium saucepan; cook over low heat 5 minutes, or until butter melts. Increase to medium heat and bring mixture to a boil, stirring constantly. Stir in sugar, vanilla, and pecans; beat until smooth and sugar dissolves. Spread Chocolate-Pecan Frosting over cooled cake.

CARROT CAKE WITH CREAM CHEESE FROSTING

Adding carrots to cake batter probably originated as an economy measure when sugar was scarce. The sweetness of carrots enhances the flavor, texture, and appearance of this large, luscious cake.

YIELD: ONE 3-LAYER CAKE

INGREDIENTS

2½ cups finely grated carrots
2 cups all-purpose flour
1½ cups sugar
½ cup firmly packed brown sugar
2 teaspoons baking soda
1 teaspoon baking powder
½ teaspoon salt
2 teaspoons ground cinnamon
4 eggs, beaten
1⅓ cups vegetable oil
1⅓ teaspoons vanilla extract

**Cream Cheese Frosting
(Yield: about 3½ Cups)**
1 (8-ounce) package cream cheese
½ cup unsalted butter
1 (16-ounce) package powdered sugar
2 teaspoons vanilla extract
1 cup chopped pecans, toasted

1 Combine carrots, flour, sugar, brown sugar, soda, baking powder, salt, and cinnamon in a large mixing bowl. Stir well. Combine eggs, oil, and vanilla; stir into dry ingredients, mixing well. Pour batter into 3 greased and floured 9-inch round cake pans. Bake at 350° for 30 minutes, or until a wooden pick inserted in center comes out clean. Cool cake in pans for 5 minutes; remove from pans and let cool completely on wire racks.

2 To make the frosting, combine the cream cheese and butter, beating at medium speed of an electric mixer until smooth. Add sugar and vanilla; beat until light and fluffy. Stir in pecans. Spread Cream Cheese Frosting between layers and on top of cake.